Taming
your
emotional
tigers

To Polly
who with love, patience
and good humour, has
endured my own negative
emotions

and in memory of
Pax
whose enthusiasm and
encouragement were the
driving force behind this book
Pax died as the book went
to press.

Taming
your
emotional
tigers

Tony Ward

inter-varsity press

INTER-VARSITY PRESS
38 De Montfort Street, Leicester LE1 7GP, England

First published 1998
Reprinted 1999

British Cataloguing in Publication Data
A catalogue record for this book is available from the British Library

ISBN 0–85111–585–3

Set in Stempel Garamond

Typeset in Great Britain by Parker Typesetting Service, Leicester
Printed in Great Britain by Caledonian International Book Manufacturing Ltd, Glasgow

*Inter-Varsity Press is the book publishing division of the Universities and
Colleges Christian Fellowship (formerly the Inter-Varsity Fellowship), a student
movement linking Christian Unions in universities and colleges throughout the
United Kingdom and the Republic of Ireland, and a member movement of the
International Fellowship of Evangelical Students. For information about local
and national activities write to: UCCF, 38 De Montfort Street, Leicester LE1 7GP.*

Contents

Why on earth?

Why on earth should a church minister write a book about feelings and emotions? Simply because, in all my dealings with people, this is one of the areas they struggle with most. Is that the only reason? Actually, no, It's also because for many years it's one of the areas where *I've* struggled most. So perhaps I should say at the outset that this book is not intended to deliver the authoritative blueprint for emotional maturity. It arises, rather, out of my own struggles, and from empathizing with the many people who have sat in my study seeking counselling and advice, in the attempt to cope with feelings that engulf them.

I confess that I have been tempted to write this book in the style of 'Follow these steps and all your problems will be solved', written by an expert who never gets overwhelmed by troublesome emotions. Maybe it would sell more copies. But it would be untrue and dishonest. I haven't yet become an emotionally mature authority on the subject. Ask my wife and my congregations if you don't believe me. I believe that with God's help I'm making progress, albeit sometimes painfully slowly.

Fear, depression, anger and failure were not things that instantly vanished when I became a Christian. In fact, sometimes my relationship with God has resulted in God opening an emotional Pandora's box that I never knew was there previously. His purpose, of course, was entirely loving – to help me to grow and mature on the road to holiness. In so doing, God has been gently coaxing me and teaching me ways to overcome my imprisonment by destructive emotions, and this book is the attempt to share something of what I am still learning myself. Christianity was once described as 'one beggar showing another beggar where to find bread'. That's the intention in writing this book. It won't have all the answers; it will contain weaknesses arising from my own limited and subjective experiences. But perhaps it will encourage fellow strugglers.

As a minister, I suppose it would seem a lot more appropriate had I written a book on something like holiness. But despite some of the excellent books on holiness that are already available, it is clear that one of the major obstacles to the growth of holiness in many Christians is an inability to know how to handle certain emotions which frequently exercise a very power-ful grip on them. When the emotional tail wags the dog, destructive patterns of behaviour almost invariably occur, and holiness remains an ever more distant goal.

Perhaps this book will help to bridge the gap because, in the end, holiness needs to be our goal. Our present subjective age is one in which there is almost an obsession with feelings. The 'feel-good factor' is not a politician's catchword for nothing! Even Christians are caught up in it. Spiritual experiences, feeling good, the 'Toronto blessing', being set free from cares, how to feel happy, are all popular Christian themes today. The purpose of this book is not the pursuit of happiness as an end in itself, but the pursuit of holiness. Sometimes, as I've discovered, the road to holiness requires the experience of emotions that are far from pleasurable. My great desire is not that this book necessarily helps people to get rid of unpleasant feelings –

because unpleasant feelings can often be necessary and instructive. It is, rather, that where unruly emotions are proving a blockage to spiritual growth and maturity, readers will be helped and encouraged in the process which the apostle Paul describes as being 'conformed to the image of Jesus Christ'.

All the feelings that are considered here have been written about very adequately and in greater depth by others. But many people who struggle with these emotions no longer have the willpower or motivation to tackle weighty books which explore at length problems such as depression or guilt. Also, many people are looking, not so much for an analytical and psychological explanation of their emotions, as for clear, practical and biblical guidelines about what to do. Counsellors and experts may thus find this book woefully inadequate. But in-depth psychology is not the aim here, for the simple reason that I am a minister of the gospel, not a qualified psychiatrist. My concern is to interpret and apply Scripture meaningfully in the pastoral-care situations that are common in every church and congregation.

There are questions at the end of some chapters, for personal application, and to facilitate setting achievable goals. Readers may benefit from reading this book in small chunks, perhaps with a friend who could act as a sounding-board and a stimulus to discussion and further thinking.

The substance of the contents was given as a series of sermons at Holy Trinity Church, Leicester, and in my previous church in Pretoria, South Africa. My thanks go to my long-suffering congregations in Leicester, and more latterly in Rainham, for allowing me the time to write, as well as to my friend Pax in Pretoria who constantly encouraged and goaded me into writing the book.

Tony Ward
Rainham, Essex

1. Taking responsibility for your emotions

Have you ever wished that God had created you with an 'off' switch? I've often thought how useful it would be on those all-too-frequent occasions when life seems to get too much, and my emotions seem to have gone into overload; if only I could just flick a switch, so that serenity would instantly return!

Of course, some people do somehow seem to switch off and put their emotions into a kind of internal deep-freeze. I met Jill a few years ago, and shortly afterwards she came to see me for some pastoral advice, as her marriage had run into severe problems. Outwardly, she was calm, composed and gave every impression of someone who had got her act together and was in control. It was only weeks later, when I was praying with her into events in her past where her memory seemed to be extremely vague, that there surfaced a tidal wave of emotional pain, anger and hurt.

Other people, by contrast, seem to live every day on an emotional knife-edge. Helen was such a person. Well-educated, with a doctorate and a responsible job, she nevertheless lived every day on an emotional roller-coaster. Highly strung, almost to the point of being neurotic, she was regularly having days off work whenever anything or anyone upset her. She seemed utterly unable to maintain an emotional equilibrium. Both Jill and Helen were committed Christians, but their differing emotional make-ups seemed unaffected by their Christian faith. Perhaps you can sympathize. The mere fact of being human means that sooner or later you are likely to have trouble with your emotions and feelings. This can happen in one of two ways – either you will find yourself overpowered by them, or else you will have found a way to repress them altogether. The problems appear instantly when the emotional tail wags the dog, but when feelings are buried and repressed, the problems often emerge only years later.

Not surprisingly, then, both of these extremes of emotional experience are unhealthy. Not to be in touch with our feelings is not to be in touch with life. But to feel too much is to be overwhelmed and drowned in a raging sea of emotion.

Sadly, as was the case with Jill, some Christians have gained the impression that if they are to live the Christian life success-fully, they must get rid of all feelings, particularly those which could in any way be construed as negative. Ruth Fowke tells the story of a mother who tried to make her sensitive son less upset by criticism by teaching him to repeat: 'Sticks and stones will break my bones, but words will never hurt me.' She made him repeat it incessantly every day, when he returned from nursery school. He would utter the words fiercely, in a vain attempt to convince himself that his feelings were not hurt, but it never worked.[1] Denial of your emotions never equips you to deal with distress. The consequence of this teaching was that this little boy came to believe that whenever he was upset at being teased, he was failing to reach his mother's standard, and was therefore 'bad'. An inferiority complex set in, and he came to regard the experience of all emotions as bad. Regrettably, some Christian teaching, when badly presented, reinforces these destructive self-attitudes. For example, have you ever heard a preacher convey the message that if you are depressed or sad, this is un-Christian? That idea is utterly wrong, and is based on Stoicism, not Christianity.

But many Christians have nevertheless ended up believing that to feel strong emotion is always bad. This is especially so if the feeling in question is an unpleasant one, such as anger or depression. But, as Dr Lawrence Crabb has helpfully pointed out in his book *Understanding People*, it is simplistic to conclude that all pleasant emotions are positive, and all unpleasant ones are negative. The feelings associated with what we would deem to be an unpleasant event are not necessarily negative themselves, just because the event is so. The death of a loved one may classify as a negative event, but the grief that ensues is not a negative emotion. It may be unpleasant, but, if the expression and length of the grieving process are normal, then, using Dr Crabb's model, the grief ought to be viewed as appropriate and constructive. The Bible itself explicitly points out that there is a time to weep as well as to laugh (Ecclesiastes 3:4).

In fact, another case in point is the very process of becoming a Christian. Such a process involves the necessary step that the Bible calls 'repentance'. Repentance is not merely an intellectual acknowledgment of our wrongdoing before God; it ought rightly to touch our emotions. Grief, sorrow, depression and despair are all displayed by the Psalm-writers when expressing their repentance towards God. Since the Bible emphasizes how important genuine repentance is, it certainly wouldn't do to label such emotions in these circumstances as 'negative'. They are entirely constructive.

Dr Crabb concludes: 'Emotions . . . can serve as a warning light telling us to take a look inside or as an indication that we're on track in our efforts to function properly.'[2] The difficulty we have is knowing when to express our emotions and when to restrain them.

Not only does the tendency to want to suppress emotion occur among some Christians, but also it is linked very much to cultural conditioning, particularly, for example, the western world's perception of the qualities that command respect and admiration. It is considered quite acceptable to scream, shout and get excited when watching the Cup Final at Wembley, but on most other occasions the uninhibited expression of emotions is frowned upon. Perhaps you have been conditioned yourself from childhood to keep your emotions under tight control. You've been told that 'big boys don't cry', or that to get angry is unacceptable behaviour. You have been taught that to express emotion is a sign of weakness. What other people will think is, in fact, one of the most fear-inducing thoughts that there is, and leads us to avoid, wherever possible, any acknowledgment or expression of our feelings. As a result, many people, rather than being imprisoned by their emotions, have instead buried them, so that they are now no longer able to feel at all.

The role of thoughts in producing emotions

You can't live without emotions, but equally you can't live *by* emotions. This is the other extreme. Since our emotional make-up, along with the rest of our humanness, has been tainted by sin, indulging some of our emotions can be very unhealthy. I meet many people who have given up any attempt to be in control of their feelings. When challenged about a violent temper, they simply shrug and say, 'There is nothing I can do about it,' or 'It runs in the family.'

In such cases, legitimate feelings can easily become destructive if they are allowed to get out of control, and damage our relationship with God or with others. Now here we have to define our terminology carefully, because it could justifiably be argued that all talk of controlling our feelings is nonsensical. Surely all our feelings are outside our control? We can't stop feeling to order! Even burying our feelings doesn't make them go away. They almost invariably surface elsewhere in a different guise. That scarcely constitutes control of our feelings.

All this may be true up to a point. Nevertheless, it is not

impossible to exercise discipline over one of the main factors that fuel our feelings – namely, the way we think. Many of the inappropriate or destructive emotions we experience are the consequence of our beliefs, and those beliefs or thought processes can certainly be examined and, if need be, changed with the help of God. As James Dobson concludes, 'emotions must always be accountable to the faculties of reason and will'.[3]

Perhaps this is why the Bible directs its message at our *minds*, rather than at our emotions. Our thoughts can unleash tremendous power upon our feelings. Writing to the Christians at Rome, Paul urges them to 'be transformed by the renewing of your mind' (Romans 12:2). Similarly, he urges the Philippians to have the same attitude (or mindset) that Jesus had (Philippians 2:5). In other words, a person's character and emotions are unquestionably shaped and influenced by their thoughts. People tend to feel what they think. How important it is, therefore, to ask ourselves some searching questions about the contents of our minds. Are we thinking rightly and appropriately? For our emotions cannot determine the rightness or otherwise of how we feel. John Stott points out that the mind is meant to stand censor over the emotions. He takes love as an example:

What should we say to a married man who confesses that he has fallen in love with another woman, that he cannot help himself, that this is 'the real thing', and that he must divorce his wife? I think we would have to say: 'Wait a minute! You are not the helpless victim of your emotions. You have accepted a life-long commitment to your wife. You should (and can) put this other woman out of your mind.'[4]

The same is surely true with 'compulsive' anger, or fear, or any other dominating emotion. God has given us the capacity to choose what content we wish to feed into our minds. Our emotions, which are much less under our control, generally take their cue from what we are thinking. If my mind is set, for instance, on being peaceable, angry feelings will make less headway than if my mind is dwelling on vengeful and aggressive thoughts. If my mind focuses on thoughts that are calm and relaxing, feelings of stress and tension will be denied the fertile breeding-ground they need to multiply.

One vital factor, therefore, is to have thoughts that are right and appropriate. The Bible calls this 'truth'. For example, Paul wrote: 'Finally, brothers, whatever is *true*, whatever is noble, whatever is right, whatever is pure, whatever is lovely, whatever is admirable – if anything is excellent or praiseworthy – *think about such things*' (Philippians 4:8). We can therefore feed our emotions with good nutrition or bad, depending on how disciplined and rational our thought life is. Emotions are fed by the things we continuously say to ourselves, and, if those things are negative, inaccurate or not based on truth, before we know it, our feelings begin dictating to our personality and behaviour in a destructive way.

I recently had the opportunity to have a 'flight' on a Boeing 757 simulator. The three-dimensional graphics, coupled with the realistic movements of the simulator, make it an incredibly authentic experience. When the flight instructor is able to effect an engine failure on take-off, or a flap malfunction on final approach, it is not surprising to me that many pilots who regularly fly the real aircraft, emerge from that simulator thoroughly drained and dripping with sweat. Just trying to make a normal approach and landing myself was not a little frightening. And yet, rationally, you could tell me that to experience such an emotion was just plain silly. I was in no danger whatever. A simulator can't crash! But my emotions were simply responding to what my mind perceived to be reality. Only by disciplining my thoughts – reminding myself that I was on a simulator, and consciously overriding what my senses told me, was I able to ensure that I didn't panic.

Emotions are fed by the way in which our minds interpret events and therefore the things we say to ourselves. Our feelings, then, not only determine our actions; they also in turn feed our thoughts. Thought processes give birth to feelings, but the feelings also serve to maintain and fuel the thoughts. It's a never-ending cycle. The more negatively we think, the more negative feelings begin to take root. How absolutely crucial it is to discipline and train our minds to think the right thoughts! In the words of Dr Lawrence Crabb, 'we must look carefully at how we think, what we think, and how our thinking can be renewed'.[5]

There are other factors, of course, which influence our feelings. A complex variety of medical, physiological and psychological factors contribute to our own particular emotional patterns. Physiologists have demonstrated how many of the emotions we experience are merely an awareness of our body's physiological changes enabling us to cope with a threatening situation. When coming in to land on that flight simulator, my heart was beating at twice its normal rate, and I suspect my body was producing a surge of adrenaline. In this sense, emotion is basically a healthy mechanism designed for our own protection. Our age, health, personality and a host of other factors will all have a major bearing on how we experience our emotions. Feelings and emotions themselves are only the end product of a chain of events, circumstances, expectations, attitudes or beliefs. It is thus vitally important that the messages which feelings convey are accurately heard before they can be managed.

But while we cannot always do anything about our physical make-up or life's events and circumstances which cause many of our emotions, we *are*, with God's help, able to shape our expectations, attitudes and beliefs. Not surprisingly, the Bible attaches tremendous significance to our beliefs and their power to influence us. When we believe truths as powerful as those contained in the Christian gospel, we are conditioning our minds with faith, hope, love, forgiveness and other positive attitudes which inevitably affect how we feel.

1 Taking responsibility for your emotions

Whatever captures our minds will end up capturing us. The thoughts of our minds affect the extent to which we will be happy or miserable, composed or angry, relaxed or tense. Realizing this, the implications for bringing balance and control into our emotional make-up are far-reaching. If, by the power of Christ, I can experience what Paul calls 'the renewing of the mind', then my priority should be to think thoughts and nurture attitudes that are true and biblical. The result will be emotions that are more appropriate and Christlike. If my thoughts are based on pride, speculation, fear, resentment, prejudice and suchlike, there will be an inevitable emotional fallout bringing with it a lot of confusion and unhappiness.

Emotions can be changed

The most encouraging conclusion from all this is that our emotional reactions are not permanent and unchangeable parts of our personality. They rather emerge out of the way we interpret events, and the way in which we see ourselves, others and God. Our beliefs, values and attitudes influence our emotional reaction in very much the same way as a rudder influences the direction in which a ship will sail. If our rudders are used properly, they can, in fact, be used to transform the negative influences of the wind and the current into something positive.

Simon Peter, Jesus Christ's disciple, discovered this one dark and stormy night. Terrified not only by the storm, but also by the sight of what he took to be a ghost on the water, Peter sought reassurance that it really was Jesus by saying, 'Lord, if it's you, tell me to come to you on the water.' Peter was a highly emotional man, who often spoke before he thought. But Jesus nevertheless invited him to come. Believing the word of Jesus, Peter found his fear replaced by a remarkable boldness. Defying the circumstances, he acted accordingly, and stepped out on the water. His belief totally transformed his trembling emotions. Fear was replaced by courage. There was a renewal of his mind.

But then came the hiccup: he looked round and saw the stormy waves, and his thinking-pattern suddenly reverted to what it used to be. His mind then told him that what he was doing was humanly impossible, and instantly the fear returned. Can you see the principle here? Our emotions and resulting actions will be changed only when our thinking-pattern is changed – or, to be more accurate, when our thinking is *exchanged*. People are constantly trying without success to change their unhelpful habits. But Christianity is not a self-improvement project. It is the exchange of our sinful, powerless and spiritually dead lives for the holy, powerful and victorious life of Christ. And that exchange must include the mind. In 1 Corinthians 2:16, Paul speaks of having 'the mind of Christ'. And that will happen to us only as we feed our minds with the thoughts of God. The importance of memorizing and familiarizing ourselves with the objective truths of Scripture can scarcely be overemphasized. James Philip rightly states: 'It is always true that, in a time of need, a mind well stocked with the teaching of the Word and with biblical principles is in an immeasurably superior position to one that is not.'[6]

In stressing the importance of allowing biblical truth to penetrate our minds, I want to make it clear that merely knowing and reciting favourite verses can very easily become a dead formula. That solves nothing, and serves only to bury the destructive feelings and divert us from our intended destination. Formulas can be dangerous, and in looking for practical steps to take we must beware of thinking that handling thoughts and feelings can be reduced to a simplistic healing technique.

A strategy, however, is very different from a formula. It's a carefully thought-through plan of action. We do not seek a definitive set of rules that ignores the complexity of our human make-up and reduces God to being a genie of the lamp. Rather, we seek a pattern based on Scripture where God works in partnership with us, building a relationship with him whereby he can challenge faulty mindsets and develop a spiritual maturity that reflects a deepened dependence on him. It takes courage, it takes time, it takes effort. Formulas look for instant, painless results. Strategies acknowledge that healing and maturity come through a process, a journey, and that God is in control, not us. Let the journey begin.

Notes

1. Ruth Fowke, *Coping with Crises* (Coverdale House, 1976), p. 28.
2. Lawrence Crabb, *Understanding People* (Marshall Pickering, 1988), p. 184.
3. James Dobson, *Emotions: Can You Trust Them?* (Hodder and Stoughton, 1982), p. 11.
4. John Stott, *The Contemporary Christian* (IVP, 1992), p. 126.
5. *Understanding People*, p. 130.
6. James Philip, *Up Against It* (Christian Focus Publications, 1991), p. 5.

2. Forget the short-cuts

When we seek to tackle destructive emotions, the temptation that will most frequently present itself is to think we have discovered a short-cut. Some Christians latch on to a prescribed programme of more intensive Bible reading and self-discipline. This may be a Christianized form of behavioural therapy. Others will seek a ministry of inner healing to deal with deeply buried inner hurts and self-protective attitudes. Still others may receive counselling that adopts the principles of 'cognitive therapy', which is concerned with the way you think about things, encouraging you to challenge prejudiced ideas or irrational thinking.

All of these may be part of the answer, and this book will try to draw on the helpful insights of each. But the important thing to recognize constantly is that there is no short-cut. As far as these techniques are concerned, many would testify that they have been there, done that, got the tee-shirt – but still have emotional problems. Without the ongoing, trusting, dependent relationship with a loving Father God, these 'fast-track' solutions lead to dead ends. They may temporarily alleviate symptoms, but they don't in themselves build trust and dependence on God. That is the ultimate key to resolving emotional difficulties.

Three principles to aim for

The strategy or pattern which I have found helpful contains three principles to aim for: repentance, repudiation and replacement.

Take *repentance* first: where our minds have been dwelling on thoughts that are negative, attitudes that are geared to self-protection, and beliefs that are speculations or have no basis in truth, an acknowledgment of sin is called for. With the admission that such thoughts are wrong comes the recognition that we are dependent on God for forgiveness and the renewal of our mind by the power of his Holy Spirit.

We're not talking about personality defects here. The Bible's definition of sin is something much deeper and more serious than that – which is why self-improvement programmes or positive-thinking techniques are woefully inadequate. Nothing less than Christ's death on the cross was sufficient to deal with the problem of sin, and our strategy has to begin with that recognition.

Secondly, *repudiation*. This entails consciously renouncing any distorted mindset and cancelling the validity of wrong thoughts. Acknowledging the fact of our sin is not sufficient to effect a lasting change. Genuine change will involve a conscious disowning of wrong motives and the sinful inner beliefs that hitherto have gone unquestioned.

Thirdly, *replacement*. This is where our thinking is exchanged, as I mentioned earlier. Memorizing relevant Bible verses to counter the error in your mind is part of it. But, to quote Dr Crabb again, 'A renewed mind involves far more than memorizing Scripture or meditating on biblical truths, although both are good and desirable . . . Real change means change in the inner man.'[1] A certain measure of personal responsibility is entailed here. Dependence and trust in God for renewal of our mind are not passive responses. Active obedience is the corollary of reliance upon God.

In fact, using a similar framework, Dr Crabb highlights repentance, belief and obedience as the ingredients for growth to emotional maturity.[2] However you choose to classify them, these three principles go together. Sadly, many of the counselling strategies employed today don't always maintain the combination.

Cognitive therapy can be helpful in determining whether our beliefs and thinking have gone awry, but without a solid biblical foundation, it can leave the issue of repentance untouched. It merely promotes a 'power of positive thinking' philosophy. Behavioural therapy also has its shortcomings, even when applied in a Christian context. More disciplined Bible reading and prayer can sometimes serve only to help one more effectively to deny the existence of emotional problems rather than to address them.

The ministry of inner healing can helpfully deal with painful feelings which have their roots in the past. But yesterday's trauma has often shaped today's habitual attitudes and thought patterns, and healing of past memories doesn't always result in a change of mindset in the present.

Renewing of the mind is a deep and ongoing work of the Holy Spirit with our active co-operation. Unfortunately for us, this transformation of the mind does not occur instantly the moment we become Christians and place our faith in Christ. The 'new creation' that the Bible speaks about in 2 Corinthians 5:17 refers to our spiritual identity, not to our behaviour, emotions or thought patterns. These things have to follow through our daily co-operation with the Holy Spirit.

Thoughts from the flesh

This transformation is an ongoing battle because the natural human mind seems to have a bias towards thinking in a distorted or unrealistic way. Left unchallenged, this tends to perpetuate

2 Forget the short-cuts

self-defeating emotional behaviour. The Bible constantly warns us against allowing our lives to be ruled by 'the flesh'. Christians do not suddenly find themselves miraculously made immune from their sin-tainted human nature. We can frequently continue to believe the most ridiculous ideas. These may have been deeply engrained in our minds for years without any basis of truth whatever. It is difficult to discriminate between beliefs that are rational, and those that are distorted by the flesh or are seemingly irrational.

A clue which points us in the right direction is the recognition of thoughts which begin 'I must', or 'I ought to'. More often than not, these are unrealistic beliefs which relate to our competence or ability, and it is these that engender emotional feelings such as guilt, or depression, or fear. Here are some of these unrealistic beliefs:

'I must earn happiness.'

'I must never make a mistake.'

'I can't really trust anyone.'

'I ought to do better.'

'I can't please God.'

'It always happens to me.'

'If I avoid problems and unpleasant situations, they will disappear in time.'

'I just don't have the will-power; I can't.'

'I can't afford the time to take a walk, read a book or relax in the garden.'

'I know that if people get to know the real me, they will not like me.'

'I must achieve great things and show myself to be perfectly competent in all I do if people are going to respect me.'

'The less I disclose about myself, the better off I will be.'

'Love does not last.'

'I must be able to control every situation in my life.'

'If I ever begin to release my emotions, I know I will lose control.'

'This is the way I am, and I will never be able to change.'

'I must invariably experience pleasure rather than pain.'

Typically, these beliefs originated in our childhood. They are perhaps the result of unhappy experiences with parents or authority figures who to some degree have conditioned the way we perceive things. At face value, such beliefs may seem plainly irrational, but usually there is a rational motivation hidden behind them. They often reflect an overdeveloped instinct for self-protection, security or the need to be strong.

So, when my feelings are haywire, my mind is in confusion and my thoughts are sinful or unreliable, and they each affect the other, where do I turn? Well, at least I have the will to turn to God and ask his Spirit to get to work on my feelings, my thoughts and on me. But let's be clear, this is no easy task. There's no quick overnight solution. My will needs to be engaged with the help of the Holy Spirit, so that I can challenge these beliefs with all my mental ability.

Where I am able to recognize and challenge the unrealistic, untrue and often unachievable nature of my beliefs, so that I stop expecting their fulfilment or condemning myself for my own humanness, then with the Holy Spirit's help I will eliminate the most powerful trigger of my problem emotions. The Bible tells us to 'take captive every thought to make it obedient to Christ' (2 Corinthians 10:5). This is hard work, but the strategy I mentioned above is an effective way to begin doing it.

Thoughts from the devil

You could be forgiven for thinking that your mind is a battlefield. It is. C. S. Lewis's classic book *The Screwtape Letters* admirably demonstrates how Satan cunningly works to maintain a grip over the way we think. The devil knows that if he can influence our thinking, then not only our actions but our faith in God will be affected. No wonder this is a major target of demonic attack. Fortunately, the help and power of the Holy Spirit are provided so that we can fight back. If you have ever had any contact or involvement with the occult before coming to Christ, your mind is likely to be particularly vulnerable (and these contacts need to be specifically confessed and forsaken). But the Bible speaks about spiritual armour that is available to protect us. One of these items of armour is the helmet of salvation (Ephesians 6:17). The role of a helmet is to protect the head, and it's within our head that our thinking takes place. So this piece of armour is designed to protect the mind. The apostle Paul says we are to 'put on' the helmet of salvation, so clearly he is indicating that some positive action is required.

Prayer is the first positive action by which this armour is put in place. It is through prayer that the truths and promises of God's Word take effect in our lives. The focus of prayer needs to be positively Christ-centred, not negatively focused on the demonic. Worship, thanksgiving and praise form the content of truth with which to fill our minds. 'Do not be anxious about anything, but in everything, by prayer and petition, with thanksgiving, present your requests to God' (Philippians 4:6). Inappropriate feelings of anxiety can be countered by the practice of thankful, worshipful prayer. It may sound an obvious, almost clichéd thing to say, but the truth is still amazingly overlooked. Anxiety focuses on one's own inadequacy, whereas authentic prayer will concentrate on God's abundant adequacy.

There is a trend today to try to engage spiritual powers in prayer and cast out demons of fear, or guilt, or depression, attributing every troublesome emotion to a demonic spirit. Spiritual warfare is real, but the biblical truth is that the ultimate battle has already been won on the cross by Jesus Christ. Our victory lies in appropriating his victory, not in engaging in personal crusades against the devil. Leanne Payne is very helpful in making this point:

> The person who adheres to such a theology and psychology will treat every sin and motion of the soul having to do with

suffering as an occasion for contending with a demonic entity. This is what has happened with the practice of 'casting out' what amount to perceived character traits and deficiencies as though these were demons rather than sins to be confessed or deficiencies to be remedied through prayer.[3]

The perspective of biblical truth is one in which Jesus is at the centre, and we are not striving *for* a position of victory, but *from* a position of victory. It is this kind of prayer which protects our minds with the helmet of salvation.

Meditation is the second means of appropriating the helmet over our minds. I am not referring to transcendental meditation here, which is based on Eastern philosophies and seeks to empty the mind. Christian meditation aims to focus the mind on biblical truth. To begin with, it's helpful to reflect regularly on how, as Christians, we participate in the victory that Christ has won. We can be confident in the truth of Ephesians 2:6 that Christ's position of supremacy and authority over every spiritual enemy is something that we share by virtue of his Spirit of power living in us.

If the reality of that seems remote, it may be because we still have to learn to appropriate what is rightfully ours. Regularly turning such truth over in our mind can help that process. This is not merely the power of positive thinking, but a reality of being identified with the risen Lord. James Philip gives a helpful analogy in his book *Up Against It*:

Like a policeman on point duty at the centre of the city, who stops the traffic by the raising of his hand (bearing the authority and majesty of the law), we may also (through Christ's authority given to us to use) stop the flow of unholy traffic through our minds and hearts – whether evil and unhallowed thoughts, doubts and questionings, fears and dreads of different kinds, or any other malevolent wile of Satan.[4]

2 Forget the short-cuts

Not only that, but the whole thrust of the Bible's teaching is to enable us to realize at the deepest level of our being that God accepts us in Christ. In his first letter to the Corinthians, Paul wrote: 'By the grace of God I am what I am' (1 Corinthians 15:10). Here's a man who knows that despite all his weaknesses, shortcomings and failures, God accepted him and loved him. The recognition that through the humanity of Jesus, God not only knows and cares, but fully understands, is one of the first steps in the healing of our distorted thinking and unwelcome emotions. The fact that Jesus understands not only the way we think, but the way we *feel*, is good news indeed. Hebrews 5:7 points out that 'During the days of Jesus' life on earth, he offered up prayers and petitions with loud cries and tears to the one who could save him from death.' There's the proof of a God who identifies with us in totality. Focusing our minds on that truth is a powerful antidote to distorted thinking.

When we meditate on how Jesus was tempted by the devil in the wilderness, when we think about his betrayal (prompted by the devil; John 13:27), and how he was subsequently deserted by the disciples, and when we see him hanging on the cross feeling abandoned by his Father, we begin to realize that he has experienced the same feelings as we have. He knows what it is like to weep tears, to be overcome with grief, to feel acute loneliness. He has wrestled with feelings that threatened to tear him apart. This is part of the miracle of the incarnation: God knows and has experienced the full intensity of the devil's assault on the mind and can therefore identify and feel with us. But more than that, he can supply the grace and the power for those crippling thoughts and emotions to be changed.

Thoughts from the world

Perceptions drawn from the world are another of the many factors that are important in the formation of our thoughts and in influencing our emotions. The way we think about things is very often related to our perceptions of others and even of God.

Cultural norms, parental opinions and peer pressure all play a part in shaping the way we think. These are not necessarily wrong nor anti-Christian, but it's helpful to examine their validity, especially if they are generating questionable attitudes or feelings.

A few years ago, a colleague of mine in South Africa was preaching an evangelistic sermon to a black congregation by means of an interpreter. One of the texts he quoted was Romans 3:23, 'For all have sinned and fall short of the glory of God.' Unfortunately, the local interpreter translated this as 'All unmarried mothers have sinned and fall short of the glory of God.' The preacher discovered this only at the end of the sermon when, in appealing for commitments to Christ, the ever-helpful interpreter took it upon himself to usher all the unmarried mothers to the front of the church! Quite how he made the equation that the definition of a sinner is an unmarried mother could be understood only if you knew something of his cultural and religious background. But it illustrates how perceptions can cloud our thinking, and consequently our feelings and attitudes.

Most people's perception of God has been shaped by a variety of things such as parental relationships, life experiences, and teaching from the church. These mental pictures of God may not always be accurate, and this explains a great deal about emotions such as guilt and fear. Let me briefly elaborate. If our perception of God is a caricature – perhaps that he is a demanding perfectionist who is always upping the stakes – then not unnaturally this will tend to breed feelings of resentment, guilt and depression within us. The desire for holiness is a legitimate aspiration, but a neurotic striving after perfection can drive many Christians to the brink of emotional and spiritual collapse.

Likewise, it's possible to have caricatured perceptions of other people, or categories of people, such as those of a different race or nationality, or those in a particular age bracket such as teenagers. Where such a caricature is negative, it's often referred to as a prejudice. Such unreasonable prejudices easily induce unpleasant feelings which can be very hard to control.

In reality, it is not the facts about a person or a situation that determine how we react, but our perceptions of them. The way we perceive someone or something may be quite different from the objective reality. We must always therefore allow for the possibility that others may perceive things differently. If we exaggerate a disaster out of all proportion, or interpret all criticism as destructive and vindictive, we shall find it hard to prevent emotions and feelings from dictating the way we react.

To summarize: the world, the flesh and the devil can all influence our thinking, and therefore our emotions. If we are going to learn how to reduce our destructive emotions, it will entail a very careful monitoring of our thought life. The great preacher Martyn Lloyd-Jones has wisely identified the ultimate cause of trouble with our emotions as 'listening to yourself instead of talking to yourself'.[5] Whatever the nature of the emotional baggage that you are trying to grapple with, aim to exert some discipline on the way you think by addressing the truth of Scripture to your mind. Even if we can't change anything else, we can challenge the thought patterns of our minds. A strategy of 'repentance, repudiation, replacement' in co-operation with God's Holy Spirit is a powerful means of harnessing those runaway emotions.

I think, for example, of a young student called Karen who corresponded with me for some time, frequently putting down on paper the feelings she couldn't put into words. Having been helped to adopt a similar action plan to that outlined above, she wrote back to say:

God has been doing so much in my mind this week! My feelings continue to be so improved and are maybe even wavering less, not more, as time goes on . . . I really do see the need now to keep feeding my mind with Truth. By giving me just one Bible verse you have provided me with a real focus for God's power. You have put a spiritual sword in my hand and taught me to fight. Part of me still seems to believe that all this is just play-acting, but I know deep down that it really is real because the change in my emotions is so very, very real. It is so wonderful. I can hardly believe it (I have long been an adherent of the 'Nothing wonderful ever happens to me' school of thought), but I know it is real, and the power of that Bible verse keeps working time and time again in some inexplicable way which goes beyond the battles in my mind. I can hardly believe I am writing all this so unreservedly! Part of me wants to call the change of emotions the result of a bang on the head, or hormones playing tricks on me, or that I've finally gone crazy. But really I know that it is God working in my life. I know I have experienced something very good and very real – could it be that the creator of the universe has touched my life personally? Wow! Words fail me. I am struck dumb at the thought – it is terrifying, awesome, thrilling, it goes beyond everything. I actually want to be alive! I haven't felt like that for ages, possibly years, and now here it is; the despair has gone, I have a life and I have a future. The light at the end of the tunnel didn't just get switched back on – it came and got me!

Two years later, she continues to make progress, reporting 'much of the heaviness has lifted', and despite ongoing problems in her life, 'the dominant note is more hopeful'. Magic solutions, no, but positive change has definitely been happening. Keep going, Karen!

Maybe Karen's experience echoes a longing in your heart. Whether your emotions dominate you, or whether you have buried them away beyond reach, they don't have to be your enemy. Emotions in themselves are neither right nor wrong, but the way we express them may be constructive or destructive. Likewise, they can be pleasant or unpleasant. On the one hand, our emotions offer us the potential for experiencing the greatest pleasure and thrills which life has to offer. They provide the joy and excitement of living that no other aspect of our human make-up can provide. Conversely, our emotions have the power to cause us untold misery and suffering. God has given us the capacity to utilize our complex emotional make-up for our own benefit and for his glory, and learning how to do this will be our aim throughout this book. David Seamands comments that Christianity 'in no way relegates the emotions to a second-class status, but recognizes that wholeness must include the emotional life'.[6]

We will explore a variety of emotions such as loneliness, depression, anger, fear and guilt – emotions we habitually tend to classify as negative. But in some cases, as we shall see, they can be wholly appropriate. It is only when such emotions drive a wedge between ourselves and God or between ourselves and others that they become destructive. Where you recognize that this has happened to you, I hope this book will help you to understand more fully God's provision for healing and restoring the damage that life may have inflicted upon you.

Notes

1. Lawrence Crabb, *Understanding People*, pp. 129–130.
2. *Understanding People*, p. 187.
3. Leanne Payne, *Restoring the Christian Soul* (Kingsway, 1991), p. 214.
4. James Philip, *Up Against It*, pp. 206–207.
5. D. Martyn Lloyd-Jones, *Spiritual Depression* (Pickering and Inglis, 1965), p. 20.
6. David Seamands, *Putting Away Childish Things* (Victor Books, 1982), p. 103.

For personal study or group discussion

1. Are you the kind of person who represses emotions, or that is ruled by them? In either case, try to identify and then jot

down events in your life that might have brought this about.

2. Is it God's intention that we should never feel sadness or anger or other emotions generally labelled as negative? If not, why?

3. Can you identify in yourself any of the unrealistic thought patterns mentioned in chapters 1 and 2? Find a relevant Scripture truth and put into practice the 'repentance, repudiation, replacement' action plan.

4. To what extent, if any, should becoming a Christian affect a person's temperament and personality?

5. Meditate on 2 Corinthians 4:7–9, 16.

3. 'Alone is when you hug a pillow'

To me, Llewellin Barracks must be one of the most lonely places on earth. This was where I had to do basic military training at the outset of my army service. Although it is nearly twenty years ago now, I can remember every detail of our barrack room. But perhaps my most vivid memory was the moment every morning when the corporal emptied the day's mailbag on top of the lockers. It was the signal for twenty raw recruits to push, shove and snatch in the desperate hope that there might be a letter there addressed to them. With no weekend passes for six weeks, and only the rarest of opportunities to make a phone call, letters from parents, wives or girlfriends – indeed, from anyone – were the most welcome event of the day. And on the days when there wasn't a letter, I ached inside. The loneliness was intense and agonizing.

As with many other feelings in our lives, loneliness is easy to experience, but hard to define. Some years ago in South Africa I counselled a very lonely person who shared with me this piece that she had written. It is one of the best descriptions I've come across.

Alone

Alone is being in a crowd of people, and yet not being able to share soul to soul with one of them.

Alone is when you hug a pillow and long to be hugged back with love and warmth.

Alone is when you are the only one who notices a beautiful tree, flower, bird, mountain or sunset.

Alone is suffering sadness, joy, or excitement and knowing that nobody else feels it the same way.

Alone is sharing something with someone and finding they don't care or understand.

Alone is having an ache which doesn't give up – like having a funeral going on inside all the time.

Alone is going to sleep because the pain of staying awake is too much to bear.

Alone is finding someone who loves and cares and understands and yet having to part because God forbids it.

Alone is hearing 'I will never leave you nor forsake you', and yet never seeing or feeling the evidence of this.

Alone is praying to emptiness. I am alone – I cannot flee from it or change it. I can only end it.

Have you ever felt like that? I imagine, if you're honest, these words probably struck some chord in you. As part of humanity, all of us, at some point or other, are going to know what loneliness is. It's part of our life and there's no escaping it. So we should not be surprised if as Christians we have sudden unexpected attacks of loneliness.

Malcolm Muggeridge spent many years as a hedonist, pursuing pleasure. He later described loneliness as 'the greatest problem of our day'.

During a week-long university mission in Britain, Dr Billy Graham chose one evening to speak on the subject of loneliness, and that night saw by far the biggest crowd of any night of the mission.

3 'Alone is when you hug a pillow'

Loneliness has different shapes and guises

We live in a world filled with very lonely people, and in fact loneliness is officially regarded as being responsible for more mental disorders than any other single factor in our society today. Now of course there are many different kinds of loneliness. Your first lonely time was being born, and each one of us experienced loneliness because we were coming from the known into the unknown. It was an emotionally stressful event. Since then many of us have encountered the loneliness of childhood. One of the memories etched most sharply on my mind is sitting by myself at the edge of the school playground watching the other children play. I had no friends to play with, and I felt isolated and ostracized. But my loneliness was mild compared to that experienced by some. Boarding-school, cruel classmates, distant parents, or being a latchkey kid have made childhood the loneliest period in many people's lives.

As one grows older, those who remain single can experience what could be called physical loneliness. After all, God made us to enjoy a sexual relationship, and if you're a single person, you're going to encounter loneliness in that area. Ironically, in the church today new Christians are taught to cope with all kinds of difficulties, but rarely are they given any help in combating loneliness. And I know of many Christians whose lives were spotlessly clean and moral, but eventually waves of loneliness overwhelmed them until emptiness and sexual desires sucked them down and almost drowned their faith. There's very often a strong temptation to fill emotional emptiness through sexual involvement.

This problem can be considerably greater for divorced people, who will have experienced at some stage the thrill and excitement of married love, and it's hard for them to be content with lesser expressions. Divorce is a hugely painful and traumatic event, and the hunger for intimacy, perhaps as a solace, is often acute. This, coupled with the awful, debilitating pain of being alone, frequently generates powerful sexual feelings, and again, many Christians have fallen into this trap.

Even marriage can be lonely

The most painful kind of loneliness occurs within marriage itself. When I was grumbling about a broken relationship that occurred in my early twenties, a friend made the point to me that it's better to be lonely and single than lonely and married. It was a wise reminder that it's all too common for a married person to live in the same house with a husband or wife, and yet be emotionally poles apart. Evenings consumed by one partner's demanding job or care for the children, or the gradual failure to spend the time needed for real communication, can lead before long to one partner failing to meet the emotional needs of the other. On countless occasions I've counselled couples in marital difficulty, and one partner will say, 'We don't communicate any more.' This is the ideal scenario for the devil to come and sow the seeds of temptation and forbidden fantasies, which even the most strong-willed and self-disciplined of imaginations will find difficult to resist. As David Seamands reminds us, we should never underestimate the intricate connection between loneliness and sexual temptation.[1]

Another reason we are often lonely in today's world is that we're so busy carving out careers for ourselves, and trying to maintain a lifestyle with a multitude of activities and responsibilities, that we simply don't have time for relationships with one another. The pace of life in today's highly technological world tends to drag us away from each other.

Having lived much of my life in Africa, I've noticed that the problem of loneliness is far less acute in the Third World and rural communities where the network of family and neighbourhood relationships is still in place. By contrast, in the big urban church where I am currently a minister, we budget on a quarter of the congregation moving on every year. Modern urban life in the West has become highly mobile. But it leaves many people without roots. They are transplanted to new places where they have no family connections and no friends. As a result, people become accustomed to having numerous casual acquaintances, but very few deep friendships.

In fact, it's widely recognized now that probably the loneliest place for many is where there are lots of people around. There's no lonelier place than a crowd. The American essayist Henry Thoreau once said that a city is a place where hundreds of people are lonely together. And I suppose in the fast-moving cities of Europe and America, where faxes and computers cut down on the need for verbal communication, all these tendencies are aggravated. Is it any wonder that sometimes we simply want to get away and to be alone? But we find that when we do, we can't cope with ourselves, and we long to have even one person to whom we can open up and with whom we can share at real depth.

Then there's the loneliness which occurs when one grows older, and life undergoes far-reaching changes: children grow up and leave the nest; retirement isolates you from the colleagues and acquaintances you worked with; ill-health or impaired mobility restricts you from getting out of the house to form new friendships and new associations. Perhaps you have even experienced the tragic loneliness of losing your spouse. The combination of grief and loneliness causes a profound sense of emptiness, and few would have the foolishness or arrogance to say that loneliness shouldn't be there for a Christian.

Wounded relationships cause loneliness

Loneliness can stem from circumstances or social causes, but it not infrequently has psychological roots. When life has been shattered by betrayal, deceit, rejection or total misunderstanding, it often produces some very lonely people. Jesus had to taste that kind of loneliness. Having formed very close relationships with the twelve disciples, he was betrayed by one and then forsaken by the remainder. On the night of his arrest and trial, he said to his disciples, 'A time is coming, and has come, when you will be scattered, each to his own home. You will leave me all alone' (John 16:32). You can sense the pain and anguish in his words.

Only a matter of hours later, in the Garden of Gethsemane, Jesus said to his disciples 'My soul is overwhelmed with sorrow to the point of death. Stay here and keep watch with me' (Matthew 26:38). The horror of what lay ahead was engulfing him. He was appealing for their support and company at a moment of acute emotional stress, but they let him down. He returned from prayer to discover his three closest friends asleep. There's no question in my mind that he would have felt betrayed by them, and desperately lonely.

Similarly, for many of us, there are occasions when we are betrayed: people let us down, or even stab us in the back. If you're a leader, you tend to assume that the people following you will respect you and support you. You don't really expect to receive knives between the shoulder blades. Yet even Christians are incredibly fickle and prone to disloyalty. People in positions of leadership become ready targets for criticism and blame. Think of Moses, in the Old Testament, constantly being made the scapegoat for all the hardships the Israelites were enduring in the wilderness. No wonder there were occasions when he felt he had had enough!

Politicians know this only too well. A former President of the United States, Harry Truman, once said, 'To be President of the United States is to be lonely, very lonely, at times of great decision.' Whatever the decision, there will always be those whose response will be to criticize not only the decision, but the character and worth of the person who made it. And sadly, this can also be true in Christian leadership. So many church leaders and clergy have had their ministries broken and shattered because of what people they trusted have said and done to them. One minister I know described it as 'emotional rape', a feeling of being stripped of any form of respect and integrity.

3 'Alone is when you hug a pillow'

Any leader will inevitably feel desolated and desperately lonely when faced with this kind of rejection and betrayal.

King David was someone who knew the loneliness of leadership acutely. Psalm 13 was written out of a very deep experience of loneliness. It's quite likely that he wrote it at a time when Absalom his son was planning to usurp him, so one can imagine something of what he was feeling. And this sense of isolation and loneliness is not just on a human level; it's on a spiritual level as well. Consider the first two verses:

> How long, O LORD? Will you forget me for ever?
>   How long will you hide your face from me?
> How long must I wrestle with my thoughts
>   and every day have sorrow in my heart?
>   How long will my enemy triumph over me?

Of course, loneliness on a human level often does cause us to feel abandoned by God as well. However important it is to feel liked, respected and valued by other people, the roots of loneliness are not just social and psychological. They are also spiritual. Augustine, a leader in the early centuries of the church, wrote these classic words: 'You [God] made us for yourself, and our heart is restless until it reposes in you.'

The New Testament constantly reminds us that deep within us there is an experience of alienation – from ourselves, from other people, but fundamentally from God. Now it needs to be said straightaway that God never intended anyone to be lonely or alienated. No person is born to live in isolation. Genesis 1 repeatedly affirms that God saw each act of his creation as being 'good'. The first occasion when something was not good is recorded in Genesis 2:18, where God said that it was not good for the man to be alone. And so he made a companion for Adam, called Eve. The word 'woman' means 'someone else', someone who was separate from Adam, who would be his friend.

The cross heals broken relationships

Loneliness, then, is something that runs counter to God's will. It was Adam's sin that introduced loneliness into human experience, because that's the root cause of humankind's separation from God. There's no doubt that one of the worst consequences of sin is that it separates and isolates. Don't misunderstand me: I'm not saying that everybody who is lonely must therefore be a dreadful sinner. But the Bible teaches that loneliness (along with many other tragic results) came about as a legacy of the initial sin described in Genesis 3. A sinful nature is therefore an inherited condition, and it brings a host of undesirable consequences with it. This is where we come to the heart of the gospel. Jesus died on the cross to remove the sin which has alienated our relationships with God, with others and with ourself.

Therefore, if that spiritual restlessness that Augustine spoke of is going to be removed, it needs an encounter with the living God, revealed in Jesus Christ. And the cross is the heart of it all.

Note

1. David Seamands, *Living with your Dreams* (Scripture Press, 1990), p. 59.

4. 'I will be with you'

What possible connection is there between the cross of Jesus and the loneliness that we feel? We more commonly associate the cross with forgiveness and salvation: When we stand in front of the cross of Calvary, we discover that we are able to give Jesus the burden of our guilt and receive God's forgiveness. This is certainly what the cross is all about. Salvation begins when you personally meet God at the cross, and acknowledge your sin and receive his forgiveness. What is less well recognized, however, is that the root of many people's loneliness is a well of unresolved guilt. This is why I come back to the cross.

Some people might be tempted to dismiss this last statement as an over-the-top comment by one of these Christians who has to find a spiritual cause for everything. Guilt is certainly not the cause of all loneliness, but even secular psychology acknowledges how frequently guilt plays a part. The following extract comes from an article devoted to loneliness in *The Psychologist* magazine.

The closer you get to the truth behind your loneliness, the more able you will be to cast it off . . . Do you ever feel that you are not worth knowing? Do you feel that you must hide away from people? Do you feel as though you are in exile from the world outside?

If the answer is 'yes' to one or all of these, then your secret, emotional pattern revolves around *guilt*. You may say – proudly and truthfully – that you have done nothing to be guilty about. Yet, astonishing as it may seem, in the emotional depths of you, you believe you have. That is why you stay alone, instead of happily mixing with other people. You are preoccupied with a sense of guilt and deep unworthiness.[1]

When we carry around a burden of past mistakes and longstanding sins, it's all too easy to experience loneliness as the byproduct of hiding from others the person that we really are.

But even Christians can fail fully to grasp that the problem has already been dealt with by Jesus. They may be active in their church, live good lives, never cheat in exams or fiddle on their income tax, and be quite religious people – but some mistake, some wrong decision in the past still gnaws away at their conscience. Whatever it is, it needs to be brought to Jesus and handed over to him. He invites us to come to him, and says, 'I love you, I have compassion for you; there's no need for you to carry this guilt any more.'

That requires repentance – an acknowledgment of our mistakes and failures, coupled with the willingness to do an about-turn, thereby allowing him to direct us. And if there's any area of our lives where we are refusing to do that, or feel unable to do that, that will be somewhere at the roots of any sense of loneliness. Until we're back in relationship with the Lord, we shall not experience deep peace with God and with ourselves. So forgiveness of our sins is the first and most fundamental answer to loneliness.

4 'I will be with you'

It's only in that very personal relationship with Jesus that you begin to find your identity, and your purpose, so that if you lose your job, or your boyfriend breaks up with you, or you never get married, or you lose your friends and loved ones, it's not the end. Yes, it hurts, but if Jesus is at the centre of your life, you are no longer emotionally dependent on them for the meaning of your life. Jesus provides that. He is the only reliable source of emotional security and strength. Even if your conscious awareness of him now seems like a distant memory, your relationship with him does not depend on subjective feelings, but on the objective promises of his word: 'Never will I leave you; never will I forsake you' (Hebrews 13:5).

The book of Proverbs speaks about a friend who is closer than a brother (18:24), and I believe it's referring there to the Lord Jesus Christ. Do you remember Elvis Presley? A few weeks before he died, a journalist went to see him at one of the nightclubs where he was performing. He said to him, 'Elvis, when you started out, you said you wanted three things out of life. You said: "I want to be rich, I want to be famous, and I want to be happy." Now you're in your forties, Elvis, are you happy?'

He replied, 'No, I'm not happy. I'm as lonely as hell.'

Yet Elvis Presley was someone who was constantly mobbed by people whenever he went out in public; he always had to hide from adoring fans. He had all the money he wanted. Girls would scream and cry and tug at his clothes, and yet he said he was as lonely as hell. Why is that? What was he talking about? I believe he was talking about an inner loneliness, a spiritual loneliness. Elvis was brought up in a good Christian church; his singing began in church, but evidently he never met the Lord Jesus Christ for himself.

The fact is, you can't ever be alone once you place your trust in Jesus Christ as your Saviour. He is always there. The very last promise he made to his disciples before he ascended to heaven was this: 'And surely I will be with you always, to the very end of the age' (Matthew 28:20). He lives in you through his Spirit.

Will Jesus cure my loneliness?

Is this, then, the guaranteed cure for all loneliness? If I have a relationship with Jesus, will I always be shielded from the ache and void of human loneliness? I want to be perfectly honest here and say that I think the answer is both 'Yes' and 'No'. It would be terribly easy to dish out platitudes and say that when you come to Jesus, you need never be lonely again. I don't think that's true, any more than you could say, 'Come to Jesus and you'll never again have a common cold.' We continue to live in a fallen world, and loneliness is just one symptom of it. Being a Christian doesn't instantly eradicate everything horrible in life.

We need to remember that Jesus himself, who knew the Father more intimately than any of us, still felt lonely at times. Because he was fully human, with normal human emotions, he had a deep need for human companionship. And since Christ was perfect, the fact that he experienced loneliness indicates that this is something neither sinful nor weak. Rather, it illustrates the fact that God has created us with a need for other people, a need to be interdependent, not independent.

Loneliness need not be the result of sin on our part. We can often suffer as a result of the sin of others. I referred earlier to the most acute moment of loneliness for Jesus following his arrest in the Garden of Gethsemane, when all his disciples deserted him and fled. In a similar way, the loneliness that we feel may sometimes be due to the failures and sins of others we love who let us down.

But apart from anything else, if Christians didn't really experience loneliness, how on earth would we be able to love and care and relate to the millions of other people in this world who *are* lonely? As Paul puts it, writing to the Corinthian church, 'Praise be to the God and Father of our Lord Jesus Christ, the Father of compassion and the God of all comfort, who comforts us in all our troubles, so that we can comfort those in any trouble with the comfort we ourselves have received from God' (2 Corinthians 1:3–4). In other words, by sharing in the common sufferings of humanity (and loneliness is one of those), Christians are better able to help and encourage and care for others who face similar difficulties.

Some dos and don'ts

How should we tackle loneliness when it strikes? To begin with, here are some things to avoid.

Don't allow your loneliness to paralyse you and prevent you from exploring possible solutions. Mental paralysis eliminates hope, and that's when desperation sets in. Hundreds of thousands of people attempt suicide every year because loneliness has driven them to the point where they've given up. The Christmas season and holiday times are often the most unbearable. When people who have families and loved ones are enjoying celebrations, reunions and family gatherings, lonely people feel particularly desperate because they can't share in the joy of others. Self-pity often takes root, and with it a tendency to lose perspective. Avoid saying negative things like, 'Nobody cares. What's the point of living?' Turn to God and turn to the Bible, and let your mind absorb the truth of how valuable you are to God, and how much he loves you.

Turn also to your church. If you're not part of a church family, scour your area for a church which is really caring. They do exist, but sometimes it takes a bit of effort and perseverance. If your loneliness is verging on desperation or despair, then you certainly ought to get pastoral help or counselling. Don't make excuses; it's vital to speak to someone like your church minister, your doctor or the Samaritans.

Don't resort to bribery. I'm afraid that all too often lonely people try and fill up their loneliness by buying companionship. Various schemes and ploys are utilized in emotional bribery. Some people will do it through invitations to meals, or through continually giving gifts. At worst, it can even occur in the guise of sexual gratuities – trying to fill up the emptiness by casual affairs, by fleeting liaisons. It doesn't work.

Don't seek substitutes. Some people, of course, go down the road of alcohol or drugs, to blot it all out and forget it. They refuse to face or acknowledge their problem. Others will turn to television, videos or home computers to fill the void. This is an escape into fantasy and it's not the answer. The danger with these substitutes is that they only reinforce your isolation from the world, and become a blockage to building relationships.

Don't manipulate. Few people consciously set out to do this, but it remains true that some lonely people can be desperately manipulative. They will use all manner of moral blackmails to try to get people to fill up their emptiness. I have encountered some elderly parents who were expert in these techniques, often trying to manufacture guilt in their children. Sadly, in the long run this only served to drive people apart rather than bring them together.

Don't withdraw. While some people try to avoid loneliness by all kinds of social devices and strategies, there are others whose tactic is to isolate themselves, and you can't get close to them. In reality, they are crying out for you to get close to them, but they retreat behind impenetrable barriers so that the thing they want is the very thing they're denying themselves. They may do it by withholding love and intimacy; they don't give anything because they want to receive. Sometimes they isolate themselves by their own off-handed manner, or rudeness, without realizing that this protective device only compounds their loneliness. They don't love you, or give to you, or share with you. They want friendship but they don't give it. And by withholding communication, they're wanting you to come and say, 'What's wrong? Have I upset you? Can I help you?' It's a subtle but self-centred response. It says, 'Come to me. I have need.'

Loneliness is not incurable!

The consequence of all this is that it's very easy for loneliness to be of your own making. This sounds tough, but if you're lonely, it's sometimes because you've allowed yourself to be lonely. What I mean by that is that loneliness is a reaction to a situation. I don't think any of us consciously decide, 'I am going to be lonely'. It's subconscious; a reaction, not an action. But it is not incurable. It's not something you are smitten with and have to put up with for the rest of your life. It's something that can be dealt with. Praise God, there's a way out, made possible by Jesus Christ's action of saving us from our sins.

When we respond in faith to what Jesus has done on the cross for us, and begin to experience his resurrected life within us, the fundamental spiritual loneliness is dealt with. Now we can begin to put right the broken relationships with other people. It doesn't have to be a self-centred thing any more, because now you can reach out to others with the love of Christ. Furthermore, you can begin to allow yourself to be loved, something that lots of people find very difficult. They've built up a protective shell. Sadly, the trouble with loneliness is that it tends to set up a vicious circle. It fills us with self-pity, and makes us tense and unattractive people, thereby inviting people to reject us. This, in turn, brings more isolation and more loneliness. Loneliness turns us in upon ourselves when our real need is to be more outward-looking and to offer friendship to others.

Five steps to take

God's desire is to break that vicious circle, but he requires your co-operation. It may seem as though your circumstances cannot be changed. But your reactions certainly can. And by the grace of God you can make a number of positive decisions that will help. Here they are.

Do depend on the Lord. This begins with the recognition that no human being, however wonderful, can fully meet our needs or satisfy our desires. Many single people have a totally false expectation that if God will provide them with a marriage partner, they will find fulfilment. Fulfilment needs to be found in Jesus, because he alone can satisfy our longing for wholeness, in both a material and a spiritual sense. Once we recognize this, and depend on God to be the source of our emotional security and strength, we are in a healthier position to cultivate relationships with others which will be a blessing from God rather than a replacement for him.

Do be prepared to take risks. If you're going to be loved, you're going to have to make yourself vulnerable. Be willing to share your emotions and opinions. The chances are that you'll occasionally get hurt. All too often, lonely people have been hurt already. Perhaps you've been rejected by a friend or someone you hoped to marry. And you want to protect yourself from being hurt again. You daren't take a risk. Here's the situation where a conscious decision to take responsibility for yourself is crucial. The only other alternative is to stay as you are and carry on in your loneliness. Passive resignation achieves nothing, but to start loving people in a practical way requires a decision.

Not everybody will reciprocate, but most people respond warmly to someone who is willing to be open and vulnerable. But if you do get hurt, take that hurt to God and allow him to deal with it, so that it doesn't become a further obstacle in your life.

Do pray for a deep, close friendship. I do believe that that's a prayer that God longs to answer. He wants you not only to have a close, fulfilling friendship with him, but also to have your needs for human companionship met.

As a child, I prayed repeatedly for God to meet that longing in my heart. It took several years for the answer to come. But when I was sixteen, I got to know Tim at my church youth group. It's still a mystery to me why we became friends; we were total opposites. Tim was something of a wild, gregarious extrovert. At that stage, I was a shy, withdrawn introvert. Only God would have seen the potential for such a deep and lasting friendship which has lasted to this day. And since that time, God has multiplied the number of my friends until I almost had more than I could cope with. There's no doubt that he's changed me as

4 'I will be with you'

part of the process, but I still feel amazed at the way my prayers have been answered from all those years ago.

Do be proactive. Don't wait for friends to fall out of the sky into your lap. Try to take an interest in people. One of the first Scripture verses I ever memorized was one my parents drummed into me during those childhood years when school was a nightmare of loneliness and isolation. Proverbs 18:24 (Authorized Version) says, 'A man who has friends must shew himself friendly.' It took a lot of effort for me to learn that truth. It involved participating in groups and accepting invitations that otherwise I might have declined. It involved a willingness to listen to other people sharing their interests or their problems. It involved being trustworthy and keeping confidences. It involved spending time and making an effort.

Do be sensitive to others. It's quite common for lonely people to be sensitive themselves, and easily upset by perceived hurts from others. But it can cut both ways, and I have met some lonely people who, in an attempt to generate friendship and escape isolation, seem unaware that they are also being insensitive. It's possible to try too hard, to try to manipulate people, or to throw yourself at them in such a way as to drive them away. An acquaintance of mine still hasn't appeared to realize that the reason so many of his friendly conversations get cut short is because he talks only about his own interests and hobbies. A sensitive person will aim to discover and talk about the other person's interests and concerns. Such an approach will rarely meet with an abrupt response.

Do receive God's love through other people. Believe it or not, that's what the church is for. The basic provision which God has made for lonely people is fellowship in his church, a community of people who care for one another and are committed to one another. If you've had the inner spiritual loneliness dealt with, then the next thing God wants for you is to get really locked into the life of the church. That will help to address the level of human loneliness.

Now the picture of God's church which many of us have is probably pretty grotty – anything but a place where we're loved and accepted and where we can be free and open and be ourselves. It's the fortunate few who find that they have within their local church the ingredients of true Christian fellowship. So if loneliness isn't a major problem for you, please, please, find someone who *is* lonely and make a point of caring for them.

There's a strong emphasis on families in the church today. Fine. But the single person, the divorcee, and the widow or widower, need to find their place in the body – not just in being shunted off to do Sunday-school teaching because everybody thinks that since they are single they've got the time. Their place in the body is found in being accepted as individuals, in being loved and cared for. A single person can sometimes go for weeks without even touching another human being. Don't be afraid to reach out and hug someone, or put your arm round their shoulders. Social barriers sometimes inhibit us, and we can be afraid that such actions could give the wrong signal; but when Jesus healed people he often touched them. Sociologists tell us that touching is good for us. We need to be far more sensitive to the needs of those around us.

We can learn a lot just by looking at how Jesus dealt with lonely people. Zacchaeus was a tax-collector who was hated and despised by his fellow countrymen, and yet Jesus noticed him in the crowd, and had time to go to his house for a meal. The Samaritan woman that Jesus met at the well had been rejected by her community, but she was treated by Jesus with tremendous love and gentleness.

Above all, remember that Jesus knows what it's like to be lonely. I've mentioned the loneliness he felt in the Garden of Gethsemane, but think too of the indescribable loneliness of the cross, when for the first time in all eternity, God the Father had to turn his face away from his own Son, because he couldn't bear to look at the sin Jesus was carrying. We cannot begin to understand the depths of his loneliness when he cried out, 'My

God, my God why have you forsaken me?' (Mark 15:34). He had been cut off even from his own Father. So Jesus understands what it's like to be lonely, and he is able to help us. Quite simply, he went through the experience of being forsaken by God so that we might never have to go through that terrible experience ourselves.

Ultimately, therefore, however important real Christian community and true friendship may be in overcoming loneliness, they'll never completely satisfy us on their own. The only lasting solution is to open our hearts to the loving heart of God. Jesus says to us: 'Here I am! I stand at the door and knock. If anyone hears my voice and opens the door, I will come in and eat with him, and he with me' (Revelation 3:20). What better answer to loneliness is there than that?

If you feel that you've never really been special to anyone, then that nagging loneliness will be overcome only as you begin to grasp your 'specialness' to Father God, and realize that when you embark on a relationship with him, his presence will be with you for time and for eternity. Perhaps we can now understand a little better how David felt when he wrote:

> Where can I go from your Spirit?
>   Where can I flee from your presence?
> If I go up to the heavens, you are there;
>   if I make my bed in the depths, you are there.
> If I rise on the wings of the dawn,
>   if I settle on the far side of the sea,
> even there your hand will guide me,
>   your right hand will hold me fast.
>   (Psalm 139:7–10)

Note

1. Pamela Wray, 'Lose that lonely feeling', *The Psychologist* 43/511, August 1975.

For personal study or group discussion

1. Reflect back on your life and try and identify the most lonely experience you have had. Would the words quoted above, from Psalm 139:7–10, have made a difference then?

2. Are there any crutches or substitutes that you are relying on, instead of God, to overcome your loneliness? Jot down what changes you think are called for.

3. In what ways does the Holy Spirit help us to cope with or overcome our loneliness? See John 14:16–18. Have you had any experience of this?

4. Meditate on Luke 22:39–46 and Mark 15:33–34. Why did Jesus have to go through these agonizing experiences?

5. Is there anyone in your church or social circle that you suspect might be lonely? How can you reach out to this person? Aim to take some initial step this week.

6. Memorize Romans 8:38–39.

5. 'Why are you so fearful?'

I have to admit, as I write this, that I'm struggling with feelings of fear. In the past six weeks we have been burgled twice, with the house ransacked on each occasion. A burning cigarette has also been flicked through the letterbox in our front door. And last night, at two in the morning, I received an abusive and menacing telephone call from an unidentified person that had distinctly threatening overtones. None of which is very reassuring when you have just moved to a new town, and feel very isolated from your old friends and family. It somehow makes all the years I spent in one of the most volatile parts of Africa seem rather humdrum and serene.

I would love to be able to give the impression to everyone that I can take all these things in my stride, and am not perturbed by the sort of thing that makes other people frightened and unnerved. Surely a Christian minister should be the walking, talking epitome of cool, confident faith in God? The reality in my case is somewhat different. Of all the emotions that I write about in this book, fear is the one that I struggle with most. And over what seems like a long period of time, God has been beavering away at the process of dealing with all my insecurities.

Some of my fears go back a long way. For as long as I can remember my overactive imagination has quaked at the thought that every ache, pain or unidentified physical symptom might just be the onset of something fatal. But being young and healthy, for many years I chose to ignore my tendencies towards hypochondria. After all, such moments of panic and fear were relatively infrequent. Then, in 1991, I suddenly went down with an unexplained illness that had a variety of alarming symptoms. My white blood cell count dropped; I had heart palpitations, pains in my chest, aching in the joints and chronic depression. For weeks I fought against a rising tide of fear that I had been struck down with something serious. The eventual medical conclusion was that I was suffering from a post-viral syndrome, but at the time, the severity of the symptoms had me thinking I had little time left in this world.

Nevertheless, the emotional strain of living with fear was worse than the symptoms themselves. I became determined that this fear had to be dealt with. Wherever its roots lay, it was incompatible with the kind of life that God desired me to live. That is not to say that Christians never should be afraid; feelings of fear are part of a normal God-given emotional make-up. The aim of this chapter and the next is not to tell you how to avoid fear. There is no way to avoid fear completely. But as with all emotions, fear can be triggered by inappropriate causes and can come to dominate or be destructive. It is then that fear needs to be faced and dealt with.

I had no idea in 1991 why I had been struck down with these mysterious symptoms. There rarely is a simple or obvious explanation as to why God allows pain and suffering. The reasons have been argued and debated for centuries. One conclusion that many have rightly reached is that God can use suffering to teach us things that otherwise we might not learn. It was only towards the end of my post-viral illness that I began to

5 'Why are you so fearful?'

realize that perhaps the lesson I had to learn was how to deal with my fears. Instead of being able to bury them in an attempt to forget about them when I was fit and healthy, I was suddenly in a position where fear had become a constant daily companion. I now needed to face these fears and overcome them. While fear is a universal experience, for many people it is never intrusive enough for them to feel that remedial action is needed. But for tens of thousands of others, fear is an intolerable daily torture. Perhaps you are one such person. And if you are a Christian, you may well have discovered that a commitment to Christ does not necessarily bring about any instant or magical change in your struggle against fear.

You have a choice

But – and I hope this offers a ray of hope – God does have a strategy for dealing with your fear. Fear is not a cross that he expects you to bear. Neither is it something that God is not interested in. We know this from the way in which Jesus, on more than one occasion, dealt with fear in his disciples. In a small boat on the Sea of Galilee, when they were terribly afraid following the onset of a sudden, violent storm, he said, 'Why are you so afraid? Do you still have no faith?' (Mark 4:40). You can see how he equates fear with unbelief. And faith and fear are like magnets of the same polarity – they repel each other. Where fear exists, faith goes out of the window, and *vice versa*.

While serving in the Chaplains' Corps of the Army in Rhodesia in 1977, I was called to visit a soldier in hospital. He was a Staff-Sergeant in the Engineering Corps who had just had his leg blown off by an anti-personnel mine in the war zone. He had nominal faith, but through this life-changing and life-shattering event, I had the privilege of leading him to a personal faith in Jesus Christ. And some time later, as he was learning to adjust to an artificial limb, he wrote to me and told me how he had been deeply struck by a caption he had seen in a window which said simply, 'Fear or faith – take your choice.' The challenge of that caption helped him to overcome the enormous psychological barrier of anxiety in facing an unknown future. He had to choose which of the two was going to dominate his thinking, and therefore his life.

Fear is not usually seen as a choice. Most people view it as an emotion over which they have no control. But the command 'Fear not' occurs 366 times in the Bible. As somebody once pointed out, that's once for every day of the year, including a leap year. And God would not command you not to do something over which you had no control. Yes, our initial response to a perceived threat may be instinctively fearful, but if we continue to fear, then it usually reflects our awareness of not being in control ourselves, an inability to be in charge of our circumstances. That certainly can be frightening – unless we have already chosen to acknowledge that God is in charge of our circumstances. When we continually believe that he is lovingly in control, fear begins to lose its power. We don't have to be in control after all, because God is. Believing that fact is a choice, and it is in that sense that the degree to which we feel fear is based on the choice we make. Do we choose God or ourselves ultimately to be in charge, and to order our circumstances?

Our power of choice doesn't have to be held in helpless bondage to feelings. In fact, the choice is not made on the spot in the moment of crisis. The choice is made beforehand, in a long-term commitment and trust, so that when the crisis occurs, the sting of fear is kept within its rightful bounds by the knowledge that a loving God is in control.

If we make the *wrong* choice beforehand, fear tends to take over whenever we feel we're no longer in control of a situation. Indeed, it can begin before that point. We can easily build up preconceptions about how things are going to turn out before the event, which then allows fear and anxiety free rein. Speculation is the breeding-ground on which fear can multiply. Truth is what counts, and many's the time that our feelings have no basis of truth. Fear deals in 'What ifs?', which are purely speculative. Faith deals in the reality and truth of God's character and promises. Seen like that, the choice of faith makes a lot more sense.

But bringing my mind to unlearn a bad habit is no easy task. It often seems to be a natural breeding-ground for negative thoughts. And as some witty person said, what you brood over will be what you eventually hatch. David Watson's definition of fear is the one that I have found most accurate in my own experience: 'Fear is faith in what you do not want to happen.'[1] When our minds become obsessed with the thing that we most dread, it can sometimes become a self-fulfilling prophecy. It's as if fear prepares the ground for the very thing we most want to avoid happening. No wonder Job said, 'What I feared has come upon me; what I dreaded has happened to me' (Job 3:25). The power of faith to bring positive results is rarely contested. What many people don't realize is that faith in the negative, in what you do not want to happen, can be equally effective. And that is the kind of faith that we universally refer to as fear.

The Bible makes it absolutely clear that wherever such fears, or negative faith, may have come from, it wasn't from God. Paul writes to timid Timothy: 'God hath not given us the spirit of fear; but of power, and of love and of a sound mind' (2 Timothy 1:7, Authorized Version). And the three things mentioned here – power, love and a sound mind – are the very things that break the stranglehold of fear in us. They are the antidote. The only fear the Bible encourages us to have is a healthy fear of the Lord.

One of the earliest promises in the gospels relating to Jesus was that we should be rescued from the hand of our enemies and enabled to serve him 'without fear' (Luke 1:74). That is his desire for you, and there's no question that it can be your experience as you begin to understand the truth of the gospel.

Identifying your fears

Fear has a whole variety of different faces, and it is important to identify where the roots of fear are. What is it that you fear most in life? Is it one of the basic fears like poverty, death, ill-health, the loss of a loved one, criticism? Could it be old age? Maybe it's rejection, or the fear of failure. All of us have some fears that we have to deal with. And the person who claims to have nothing to fear at all is a liar.

Many of us wish we could identify a concrete cause of our fears – snakes, spiders, rottweilers. Then it wouldn't be so bad. But sometimes our fears aren't even recognizable, and we don't know why we respond as we do. The initial cause may be buried back in the past, in early childhood perhaps. But the fear suddenly grips us when the subconscious mind associates some current or potential future experience with some trauma from the past which our conscious memory may have forgotten. In fact, our minds and imaginations can twist us into such knots that we can get caught up in the vicious circle of being afraid of fear itself.

Yet not all fears are bad. God has designed us to have certain positive fears. For example, the Bible says that you and I are to fear the Lord: 'What does the LORD your God ask of you but to fear the LORD your God, to walk in all his ways, to love him . . . ?' (Deuteronomy 10:12). To fear God does not mean to be in cringing terror of him. Rather, the fear of the Lord is a reverence for God, a respect for who he is. But this is not an instinctive fear. It has to be taught and learned.

Similarly, another positive fear God has designed to be the norm for us is a protective fear. Otherwise we would make some very, very damaging mistakes. As with the fear of the Lord, this has to be learned. Toddlers are taught by their parents not to go near a fire, or put their hand on a hot oven. We ensure that their inquisitive fingers are not inserted into electrical sockets. Outside the home, we try to instil within our children a healthy fear of traffic, so that they don't play in the road. These are healthy kinds of fear, to protect us from those things that would endanger us. The sad fact is that most parents will teach their children to have this kind of healthy fear of fire or electricity, but they totally neglect to teach them the healthy fear of the Lord.

Note

1. David Watson, *Fear no Evil* (Hodder and Stoughton, 1984), p. 153.

6. Replacing the fear

Acquiring the kind of healthy fear I spoke of in the last chapter is a helpful start in combating negative fears. But now we need to identify some of the sources of our negative fear, and grasp the biblical antidote. Here it helps to have a spiritual understanding of our make-up, as well as psychological insights.

According to the Bible, the original cause of all negative fear was our choice not to fear God. The first time that fear is mentioned in the Bible is in Genesis 3. You will remember how Adam and Eve had been given everything they could possibly desire in the Garden of Eden. And then Eve chose to sin against God. Adam followed her, and then the Bible records the following conversation:

The LORD God called to the man, 'Where are you?'
He answered, 'I heard you in the garden, and *I was afraid* because I was naked; so I hid' (Genesis 3:9–10).

6 Replacing the fear

Sin resulted in a negative fear caused by alienation and separation from God.

This is why fear is such a widespread human experience. Human nature instinctively wants to distance itself from God, because we cannot cope with either his holiness or his sovereignty over us.

So the end result is that we now fear one another. We live in a fear-dominated society. We're afraid to walk in the streets at night. We have alarm systems, security cameras, security guards. The fear of crime is increasing every year. I can remember, even at my relatively young age, times when people didn't lock their windows or doors, and the idea of locking your car door never entered your head. But that was in a period when people had not totally lost their positive fear and awesome respect of God.

But if sin against God is the original cause of all fear in general, particular fears are normally learned or acquired by experience. I mentioned earlier that parents ought to teach their children the positive fears: fear of the Lord, and a healthy respect for things that are potentially dangerous, like electricity. Sadly, parents and relatives can also unwittingly teach their children negative fears, by projecting their own fears on to them. My grandmother was very fearful of thunderstorms and, living in Africa, we frequently experienced some particularly loud sound effects and dazzling lightning displays in the rainy season. If there had been sufficient space under the bed, I think that's where my grandmother would have taken refuge! Lightning is certainly dangerous, and certain common-sense precautions are advisable in an electrical storm. Her fear, however, was an over-reaction that had been communicated to her by her own parents and family. It was something that was learned.

Similarly, my own struggles with fears concerning my health may have been unconsciously acquired through growing up in a family where both my parents suffered chronic ill-health. Health problems preoccupied our lives, and that's how fear gained a foothold.

Another source of fear stems from the way we use our minds. Anxiety need not be related to what has happened or is happening, but is the outcome of something we *believe* to be happening. An over-fertile imagination can generate feelings of fear responding to non-existent threats. This is because our emotions are unable to distinguish between what is imaginary and what is a real or genuinely potential threat. Therefore our physical bodies respond to imaginary fears in the same way that we would respond to an actual threat.

The same is true concerning fear of the unknown. Once, in the early hours of the morning, I was suddenly awakened by a deafening thud downstairs. My imagination instantly ran riot, wondering if I was about to be murdered in my bed by masked intruders who had kicked the door down and barged into the house and were coming to get me. It could have been a break-in, but I had no idea whether my imagination was being over-fertile or whether there was a genuine threat. My body certainly reacted as if it were real. My heart began beating at a phenomenal rate, my stomach churned, the adrenaline began to flow. It was only after there had been total quiet for what seemed like an age that I plucked up the courage to investigate, only to find that the thud had been caused by a picture falling from the wall when the hook had given way.

That illustrates how frequently we are shaped not by events themselves, but by our perception of those events. Perhaps I over-dramatized the unknown 'threat' in my mind, but although my fears proved groundless, they weren't entirely unreasonable and they prepared me to take any possible action to protect my safety. It would just have been better if my heart hadn't taken quite so long to resume beating at its normal pace again!

What *might* happen

Even where the facts *are* known, it is possible to interpret them in a negative way so as to cause fear. Two people can react to the same circumstances in totally opposite ways. I'm reminded of the two shoe salesmen sent to Africa to develop markets for their company. One faxed a message home which read: 'No scope for market in this area. No-one wears shoes here.' The other salesman also sent back a fax: 'Tremendous opportunity for development! No-one wears shoes here.' Both of them saw the same facts, but their interpretations were entirely different. One was a pessimist, the other was an optimist.

This was exactly what happened when the Jews were surveying the promised land after the exodus from Egypt. Twelve spies were sent in to explore the region, do a survey and make an assessment. Two of them came back and reported how fertile the land was, and what abundant prospects were evident. The other ten reported that the land was occupied by giants. The Jews chose to be influenced by the fearful thinking of the ten, with the result that they withdrew and spent forty years wandering in the wilderness.

There is a fable about an elderly peasant farmer riding his cart into a city in India. On the way he stopped to give a lift to a frail, aged woman who climbed on to the back of his cart. During the course of the journey, the farmer was horrified to discover that his passenger was none other than a personification of the spirit of the plague, cholera. However, the gnarled old woman reassured him that only a hundred people in the city would die of cholera. As a guarantee, she offered him a dagger, saying he could strike her dead if more than a hundred perished. But when they reached the city, ten thousand people died. When the angry peasant reached for the dagger to deliver the death-blow, the aged woman raised her hand in protest, saying, 'I was true to my word – I killed only a hundred. It was fear that killed the others.'

A great deal of fear is generated by pessimistic, negative thinking – the dread of what might happen. And, in some cases, by negative thinking you can programme yourself so that the imaginary object of your fear actually becomes a reality. If you have to speak in public, and you spend hours beforehand imagining the worst, when the time comes your fear might cause those imaginary thoughts to be fulfilled. God gave us an imagination for lots of reasons, but if you're going to use it, you need to imagine what is good. The way you think will influence the way you feel. The degree to which you allow your imagination a free rein, to spend time contemplating everything that you don't want to happen, will determine how gripped by anxiety and phobias you become. Charles Swindoll wrote: 'I am convinced that life is 10% what happens to us and 90% how we react.'[1]

Another primary reason is a poor self-image. If you have the general perception that things never work out for you, that you never get the breaks in life, that you're accident-prone, and you then confront something in life that's new that you've never experienced before, you are gripped by fear. 'I can't . . . I never have been able to . . . I don't have the gift . . .' You are fearful not because you can't handle it, but because you have *decided* that you can't handle it. It's not because you don't have the power to do it, or the ability to do it, but because you have *decided* that you don't. We defeat ourselves by the attitude we have about ourselves.

There's another reason for our fears, and that's guilt. We look at the past and we see failures, and when we face the same situations again, what happens? Instead of making a new start, and seeing ourselves doing it in a positive way with the help of God and in his strength, we go back and we re-evaluate what happened in the past. And we say, 'Oh, I couldn't do that.' Why? Because we are not willing to forgive ourselves, or to trust that God has forgiven us. So guilt wipes out our faith.

The antidote to fear

In the vast majority of cases, fear is nothing more than a bad mental habit. True, there does exist a physical condition, 'panic disorder', the causes of which are still being researched. Some say there may be a physical cause for the condition, whereas others say that diet plays a part. There are drugs available for people who suffer from panic disorder, but I would also recommend the strategy outlined in Dr Roger Baker's book, *Understanding Panic Attacks.*[2] The kind of fear which most people experience, however, is rooted in the mind.

This is where it may be helpful to consider the steps outlined in chapter 1: repentance, repudiation, replacement. If our destructive fears derive from having made the wrong choice about who we trust to be in charge of our life, then the right place to begin is by acknowledging our sin and self-centredness. In the Old Testament, God challenges his people: 'Choose for yourselves this day whom you will serve' (Joshua 24:15). That same choice is presented to us today: faith or fear. Not to choose simply results in the wrong choice by default. It will be self that maintains control. But faith cannot bypass *repentance.* If our fears have been the result of thinking negatively for fifty years, that needs to be acknowledged to God, and his forgiveness received. Such bad mental habits can be broken even after many years, not simply by positive-thinking techniques, but because God is in the business of renewing minds.

Positive-thinking techniques alone can lead to denial, which is unhelpful. Grace Sheppard has written in her book *An Aspect of Fear,*

> It is important to learn to be more honest, because that frees us from living a split life, thinking one thing and doing another, such as pretending that we are unafraid when inside we are quaking. Sometimes we *have* to act like this but we must, at least privately, acknowledge how we feel. Acknowledging fear like this helps us live more honestly with other people, recognising that they too share similar feelings from time to time.[3]

If your fears have been learned or are the consequence of the sins of others, or of negative transference from others, ask God to release you from that. Perhaps you need to ask a trusted

Christian friend to pray with you. It may be necessary, secondly, to *repudiate* or renounce the influence that parents or family or other influential people have had over you, particularly during your childhood.

Thirdly, you then *replace* the fearful thoughts with the words of truth God gives us in the Bible. Memorize these truths, meditate on them, and continue to focus on them, because God's truth is powerful. Here are some of those truths about fear mentioned in the Bible:

For God hath not given us the spirit of fear, but of power, and of love, and of a sound mind (2 Timothy 1:7, Authorized Version).

Do not be anxious about anything, but in everything, by prayer and petition, with thanksgiving, present your requests to God (Philippians 4:6).

. . . so that by his [Jesus'] death he might destroy him who holds the power of death – that is, the devil – and free those who all their lives were held in slavery by their fear of death (Hebrews 2:14–15).

The LORD is my light and my salvation –
  whom shall I fear?
The LORD is the stronghold of my life –
  of whom shall I be afraid?
(Psalm 27:1)

I sought the LORD, and he answered me;
  he delivered me from all my fears.
(Psalm 34:4)

I will not die but live,
  and will proclaim what the LORD has done.
(Psalm 118:17)

6 Replacing the fear

You will repeatedly face situations which engender fear. This is where your choice is so important. 'Do not anxiously look about you,' God says in Isaiah 41:10 (New American Standard Bible). He knows that one of the keys to overcoming fear is what we focus on. I can choose to think about what awful things might happen, or I can choose not to think about them, by *replacing* such thoughts with God's truth. This will be an ongoing process, not least because my mind somehow finds it easier to contemplate all kinds of disaster and catastrophe than it does to contemplate normality and a completely trouble-free life.

So, if I'm fearful of flying, for example, my mind will dwell much more readily on thoughts of turbulence, bombs and the plane crashing than on imagining myself reclining in a seat with a cabin attendant serving me a drink that remains absolutely steady in the glass. Why? Perhaps it is simply a bad habit, the result of regularly allowing my mind to explore the worst scenario. Perhaps it is because I don't normally spend time contemplating what is uneventful and normal. I guess you're the same. Therefore, if we are going to replace the negative thoughts, it may help us if we train our imagination to bring Jesus into the situation. Thus, to continue the example of flying, focus your mind on Jesus being with you, seated alongside you. Concentrate, in whatever form is helpful, on Jesus being in control. (Some people's fear of flying relates to an inability to feel that they're in control.) It goes back to the issue of choice, as we discovered earlier. These are replacements which give your mind some equivalent imagination to play with, but of a positive, true and spiritual kind. Where you focus your mind makes all the difference. We are to focus on God, so that his power, his love, and his perspective (sound mind) act as the antidote to fear.

Clinical experts may call this 'cognitive therapy', a strategy which seeks to address the way we think about things and perceive the world and ourselves. It is designed to help us challenge any irrational ideas and fears, and thereby free ourselves from our destructive bondage. Many have found that this form of therapy goes a long way towards breaking the stranglehold of fear or panic. When supplemented by the power of God and the truths of the Bible, however, the results are far more effective.

Some Christians would say, 'You just need to receive deliverance ministry. You just need someone to lay hands on you and deliver you from a spirit of fear.' Now I believe in healing and deliverance, but all too often we want to shift the responsibility to God, when it actually belongs to us. In order to deal with fear we need faith, and often we don't want the responsibility of exercising our faith and making whatever changes are necessary in the way we live. We merely want someone to pray for us and provide instant deliverance.

There are certainly occasions when deep-seated fear has allowed demonic influence to gain a foothold, reinforcing that fear. But we must never avoid the personal responsibility for the thought patterns we have chosen to cultivate. It is all too easy to end up giving our attention to the devil by imagining what he is trying to do *to* us, rather than focusing on the Lord and what he desires to do *for* us.

Moving from fear to faith will usually – let me emphasize again – be a process. I haven't arrived myself yet. There are layers within me that probably still have to be excavated and dealt with. From time to time, I still find a wave of fear rising up within me. But God has shown me the way forward, and bit by bit, I know I'm gaining ground. I hope that will be your experience too.

Here's a prayer I came across, written by a white South African living in the volatile political situation prior to the abolition of apartheid:

I'm afraid, Lord
I'm afraid of mines and bombs and guns

6 Replacing the fear

I'm afraid of every unfamiliar sound
I'm afraid of the stranger knocking on my door
    just looking for work or food or clothes.
You taught me, Lord, to open my doors
to feed the hungry
to clothe the poor
to provide in any way I can
But now I'm afraid.

Why is it, Lord, that we need higher fences and
    more security locks and even a stronger door?
Why is it that I feel hurt by the security check
    at the local store?
Why do I feel this compassion for the young man
    in uniform?
Why am I afraid, Lord?

I pray to you
that our government may choose it wiser to go two miles
when pressed only for one
Please guide our spiritual leaders
that they may show us the smaller road
Teach us to wash the feet of our servants
to be the best in every way
I pray that you'll remove all bitterness from our mind
that black and white will go hand in hand
and everyone turns colour-blind.

I stopped praying
when I suddenly realized that I was not alone
You said to me that you'd take care
You promised to be with me
for as long as I try my best to do my share
Thank you, Lord, that you were willing to hear
Thank you for removing all of my fear.[4]

Notes

1. Quoted in Dr Bill and Frances Munro, *A Place of Rest* (CWR, 1996), p. 12.
2. Dr Roger Baker, *Understanding Panic Attacks and Overcoming Fear* (Lion, 1995).
3. Grace Sheppard, *An Aspect of Fear* (Darton, Longman and Todd, 1989), p. 33.
4. Attributed to H. Pool.

For personal study or group discussion

1. How easy do you find it to believe that God is in charge of your circumstances? If you instinctively desire always to be in control, what steps can you take to relinquish control to God?
2. What turns a natural concern or positive fear into something abnormal and destructive?
3. In what ways do power, love and a sound mind (2 Timothy 1:7, Authorized Version) break the stranglehold of fear? See Psalm 68:34–35; 1 John 4:18 and Isaiah 26:3. How does this apply to you?
4. 2 Corinthians 10:5 says, '. . . we take captive every thought to make it obedient to Christ'. In the light of these two chapters on fear, how would you go about this?

7. 'I'm a failure'

You have probably read a version of the following story before, but it makes a very telling point concerning failure.

A girl went off to college and for many months never contacted her parents. She felt rather bad about this, and eventually decided she'd better put pen to paper. And so she wrote this letter to her parents:

Dear Mum and Dad,

Since I left for college I have been remiss in writing, and I'm sorry for my thoughtlessness in not writing before. I'll bring you up to date, but before I do, please sit down. It is important that you sit down before you read on. Are you sitting down?

I'm getting along pretty well now: the skull fracture and concussion I got when I jumped out of my dormitory window (when it caught on fire shortly after my arrival) has pretty well healed. I only get those sick headaches a couple of times a day. Fortunately the fire in my 'dorm', and the jump, were witnessed by an attendant at the petrol station. He ran over, took me to hospital, and continued to visit me there. When I got out of the hospital, I had nowhere to live because of the burnt-out condition of my room. So he was kind enough to invite me to share his one-bedroom basement flat with him. It's sort of small, but very cute. He is a very fine boy, and we have fallen deeply in love and are planning to get married. We haven't set the exact date yet, but it will be before my pregnancy begins to show.

Yes, Mum and Dad, I'm pregnant! I know how much you are looking forward to being grandparents, and I know you will welcome the baby and give it the same tender love and devotion you gave me when I was a child. The reason for the delay in our marriage is that my boyfriend has an infection which I carelessly caught from him. I know, however, that you will welcome him into our family with open arms. He is kind, and although not well-educated, he is ambitious. Although he is of a different race and religion from ours, I know that your often-expressed tolerance will not permit you to be bothered by that.

In conclusion, now that I've brought you up to date, I want to tell you that there was no dormitory fire. I did not have concussion, and I do not have a skull fracture. I was not in the hospital; I am not pregnant; I do not have an infection and there is no boyfriend in my life. However, I have failed history and science, and I wanted you to see these results in their proper perspective.

I guess the story is apocryphal, but it's the sort of letter I can imagine a number of students I know sending to their parents. Expectations of achievement seem to have reached an all-time high. And as expectations increase, so do many people's sense of failure. Teenage suicides, prompted by the merciless pressure to achieve, continue to grow. Yet it is not only parents who have high expectations of their children; we are often conditioned to demand higher and higher achievements from ourselves throughout the whole of life. And when those goals, for whatever reason, are not attained, our self-esteem plummets. We feel a failure.

Failure is something we all have to face at some stage. But the emotional pain that arises from failure often cripples us. Therefore it's important to be able to put failure in its proper perspective. We need to learn how to cope with the gamut of feelings that bombard us in response to failure: inadequacy, inferiority, shame, self-pity, helplessness, resentment and blame are just a few.

Christians are certainly not exempt from becoming preoccupied with failure. If it's not academic failure, or failure in relationships, or in getting a job promotion, it can simply be the sense of failure when we find ourselves falling short of the standard or quality of life that we know God wants from us. Our failures cause us to feel unworthy of serving God or incapable of being used by him. Far too many Christian people feel that having committed some sin, it is now impossible for them to continue any useful Christian life. They slip from significance and even leadership in their church into obscurity and paralysis.

In one of the churches where I used to be a minister, there was a Quiet Room which had a prayer-request book, in which people could write their requests for prayer, anonymously if they so wished. It was interesting that so many of these requests reflected people's struggles to come to terms with failure. One request read: 'Please pray for me – I feel so confused. I used to be a strong Christian, and now all that has gone down the pan. I feel as if I'm really mucking up my life.' Another wrote: 'I want to carry on being a Christian, but at times I feel so inadequate and unable to cope with it.'

They're not alone. Even people who outwardly seem to be successful and omnicompetent often secretly agonize over their perceived failures. The church has sometimes been guilty of reinforcing these feelings of failure by preaching doctrines of prosperity and success. Christian bookshops are full of biographies featuring miracles, amazing conversions, and powerful answers to prayer. Christian magazines tell of successful churches, where 'successful' means overflowing numbers, multiple healings, abundant resources and dynamic leadership. Sometimes we are left feeling more discouraged than encouraged. The regular diet of Christian triumphalism can result in our feeling totally inadequate by comparison.

Another anonymous contributor to the prayer-request book echoes this feeling:

> I'd appreciate prayer as I feel ashamed over not being able to live out my healing. Christian counselling has given me the impression that because I should be accepting and living in my healing, I'm not allowed to tell anyone if I'm having difficulties. I feel as if my counsellors have said, 'God has healed you, now get on with it.'

Casualties of the Christian success syndrome such as this are not uncommon.

As Russ Parker points out, 'While it is true that we have the power and authority in Jesus's name to cast out demons and break down the strongholds of evil in people's lives and minds, we do not have the power to avoid failure or suffering.'[1]

Oswald Chambers once rightly concluded that the twin deceivers of the Christian life are success and failure. And grappling with repeated failure has forced me to consider more thoroughly God's perspective on success and failure.

I discovered that I was one of thousands of Christians who needed to learn that God himself is familiar with failure. The very essence of the gospel is that God has embraced the failure that's endemic to humanity. Jesus certainly experienced failure in both his living and his dying. That idea seems unthinkable to many, because they find it virtually impossible to see failure as anything other than sin. But consider – realistically – how Jesus as a young boy learned his father's trade in the carpenter's shop. Did he always produce the perfect product at the first attempt? Or did he have to learn by trial and error? If we have the idea that as an apprentice carpenter Jesus would never have produced a chair that wobbled or a door-frame that wasn't exactly true, we are possibly denying his true humanity.

Even the three years of Jesus' public ministry had its failures. For example, following some tough and (to Jewish minds) even distasteful teaching, the vast majority of Jesus' followers turned away and didn't follow him any more. With a deep sense of personal sadness, Jesus asked his twelve disciples, 'You do not want to leave too, do you?' (John 6:67). They said they wouldn't, but when the crunch came and Jesus was arrested, you couldn't see the disciples for dust. Being fully human, Jesus couldn't help but feel some sense of failure in what he'd set out to achieve.

Then the crucifixion itself shows us the Son of God identifying with human failure, and taking it on himself. As Maria Boulding points out, 'Only by embracing our failure at its starkest could Jesus heal all that failure, particularly the failure that masquerades as self-sufficiency and success.'[2] From a human standpoint, the cross of Jesus looks like an example of utter and complete failure. A form of death reserved for criminals, it's a graphic illustration of weakness, shame and humiliation – an ignominious end to a life which, for the most part, had been lived in relative obscurity.

But what the cross illustrates with such amazing clarity is that failure is often an indispensable prerequisite to success. It is out of the failure and defeat of the cross that God has fashioned the glorious victory of the resurrection. The victory would not have been possible without it. The same is true of us. If we don't take the risk of failing, we won't get the chance to succeed. It's a victory in which we share, and therefore failure need never be final. In Christ, our failures have been redeemed. Whether those failures are the result of our mistakes, or whether they're something imposed on us by other people or circumstances, doesn't matter.

That fact doesn't always make failure any easier to cope with at the time. It is still something we want to avoid if at all possible. In my teenage years and early twenties I went through the typical experience of falling in love on a number of occasions, only to find that it was repeatedly unrequited. If you have been through that yourself, you will know how utterly devastating it can be. After a succession of such 'failures', I remember praying to God that he wouldn't cause me to fall in love again unless it was with the right person. I didn't want to risk another failure. It took God some years to get me to realize that if I never again took the risk of failing, then I wouldn't get the chance to succeed. In fact, what I learned through those various failed relationships was necessary for subsequent success. Just as the cross was necessary for Jesus in paving the way for the resurrection, so failure is often a necessary step in paving the way for our eventual victory or success.

We saw in the last chapter how Satan wants to hold us in bondage to fear (which is usually related to something in the future). His other tactic is to hold us in bondage to failure (which is usually related to something in the past). If he doesn't succeed in one, he will try the other. And as we all have a past, he can generally find some failure to exploit, whether it's a failure for which we are responsible, or damage inflicted by the failure or weakness of others.

Not surprisingly, it is in our attitudes and emotions that we are most vulnerable. Failure is one of the chief culprits for bringing negative emotional fallout into our lives. And this is what we need to look at now. Our emotions can react in a number of ways. Here are some common responses.

7 'I'm a failure'

Feelings of shame and rejection

Failure very easily produces a sense of shame, particularly where we are responsible. If it is caused by something outside our control, it's hard, but it's far worse if it's the kind of failure that's preventable and results from our own stupidity. People are sympathetic when outside factors bring failure. But when it's our fault, we face people's ridicule. It can start at home, at school, or in the workplace, and it's usually the result of being labelled. It's amazing how many parents have branded their children as failures. The child is continually being compared unfavourably to an elder brother or sister.

We live under the curse of a society which says that if you don't achieve at something, you're a nobody. You have to excel at sport, or academic work, or ballet, or cooking. So we have the media reporting kids as young as nine years old blowing their brains out because they get a 'C' on their school report. We have come to think that our achievements are our identity, and society is so success-oriented that if we don't live up to the standards we think we've got to live up to, we write ourselves off as a flop.

The ensuing sense of shame and rejection can manifest itself in three ways. One is to become a compliant people-pleaser. You try to placate people and win their affection and allegiance in an attempt to reduce the terrible feeling of self-rejection and self-loathing that we call shame. Such people work desperately hard to be liked, and strive to earn acceptance and recognition. They believe they can show people by what they do that they are lovable. But they know nothing about unconditional, positive love and affection.

A second way of handling the shame of failure is to withdraw from people into aloneness. It's always sad when you meet someone who tends to reject love when it's offered for fear of being rejected once more. People who do this idealize strength. Their philosophy is 'I don't need anybody else; I don't want any relationships. I'm strong enough to do without them.' But underneath that façade they are merely avoiding those people with whom they would risk further shame and rejection.

A third response is to become a perfectionist. If my father shamed me and told me I was a failure and would never amount to anything, what do I do? Well, I become a workaholic to achieve and accomplish more than he ever did – to live in a bigger house, to have a better income, and to be seen to succeed, so that I can say to myself, 'I no longer have to feel shame.'

So how does God heal these feelings of shame? In my experience, I've discovered three steps. In the first place, God will heal our shame when we learn to think about it as Jesus does. 'For the joy set before him [he] endured the cross, *scorning* its shame' (Hebrews 12:2). When Jesus went to the cross, he experienced the ultimate in shame and humiliation. He was strung up, stark naked like a butterfly pinned to a board. He was utterly exposed in the most demeaning and dehumanizing way. But this verse says that Jesus scorned the shame. He looked down on it; he didn't rate it as worth considering.

It can be quite revolutionary when we adopt the same attitude. The process of overcoming shame begins when we start to think about ourselves as God thinks about us. Shame-filled people will tend to believe that they are basically undesirable and undeserving human beings. That is not God's opinion. For several weeks in 1992 I underwent a process, initiated by the Holy Spirit, of retraining my mind. Deeply buried roots of shame were gently excavated, and I had to let go of them and acknowledge in repentance that my thoughts about myself were totally at variance with God's thoughts. The Holy Spirit brought the realization that to God the Father I'm totally desirable by virtue of being in Jesus. Not undesirable. Not undeserving. My mind was being forced to do a mental somersault. But God's strategy for dealing with negative emotions is always to renew the mind. That's where you have to start. Where failure has led to feelings of rejection and shame, begin to think like Jesus, and dismiss those feelings as wrong and untrue.

7 'I'm a failure'

Secondly, there comes the process of letting God love us and accept us despite our sense of failure. On New Year's Day 1929, the University of California met their rivals Georgia Tech in the American football Rose Bowl. In the first half, a young man called Roy Riegels gained possession of the ball for California following a fumbled pass. But he lost his bearings and began running the wrong way. He was tackled by one of his teammates only yards before he would have scored for the opposing team.

During half-time, the California players sat in the locker room awaiting the coach's censure. Riegels sat in a corner with his face in his hands and wept with shame. Minutes before play resumed, Coach Price addressed the team. All he said was, 'Men, the same team that played the first half will start the second.' But as the players stood up to file out on to the field, Riegels did not move.

The coach said, 'Roy, that includes you. Didn't you hear me?'

Riegels scarcely raised his head. 'I couldn't face that crowd in the stadium to save my life.'

The coach put his hand on Riegel's shoulder and said, 'Son, get up and get back on the field. The game is only half over and I need you to go out there and give me the best you've got!'

Spectators at that match have testified that they have never seen a man play football as Roy Riegels played during that second half. Riegels was later quoted as saying, 'When I realized that my coach still believed in me, I could do nothing less than give him my best.'

Have you ever had an experience like that – where the shame and humiliation prompted you to give up? Be reminded that the Coach hasn't rejected you. He still loves you and believes in you. No failure is so awful that he cannot forgive us and re-equip us if we'll let him. Simon Peter, one of Jesus' closest disciples, denied him three times. After the crucifixion, Peter felt that he wasn't fit to be a disciple, and that he'd better go back to his fishing career. But Jesus met him on the beach, recommissioned him, and set him on the path to becoming one of the greatest apostles of the early church. It's the experience of allowing God to love us and accept us that causes us to let go of the shame and put our life back together again.

But thirdly, shame needs to be healed not only in our relationship with God, but in our relationship with other people as well. That's something that entails risk, but it's absolutely critical. If you have been rejected by others in the past, that risk will seem even greater. But bear in mind how Jesus coped with rejection. 'He was despised and rejected by men' (Isaiah 53:3); he came to his own people, 'but his own did not receive him' (John 1:11). And yet he didn't reciprocate that rejection. He didn't withdraw. He didn't cut himself off from people. On the contrary, he forgave them, loved them, and prayed for them. Ask for God's grace to develop the same attitudes.

If you don't want to be permanently imprisoned by failure, try to find Christian friends who will say, 'No matter how much you struggle, no matter how much you fail, no matter how you feel, we accept you.' Seek a group in your church who will affirm you in that way and stand with you while God continues the healing process. If you're not fortunate enough to belong to a helpful church, make it your aim to nurture a Christian friendship with one other person with whom you can be honest and open about yourself. Perhaps you will be able to support and encourage each other. And don't consider yourself an even greater failure if you can't achieve this overnight. Sometimes our sense of failure stems from expecting too much too soon.

God is not willing that our failures and shame should win the battle, and he encourages us to start the journey to healing with those three steps: beginning to think as Jesus does and scorning the shame; letting God touch us with his love and acceptance; and findings a network of supportive friends with whom to share our shame.

Notes

1. Russ Parker, *Free to Fail* (Triangle, 1992), p. 28.
2. Maria Boulding, *Gateway to Hope* (Fount, 1985), p. 69.

8. Child of a loving Father

I think the greatest enemy to living as Christ intended is bondage to guilt – that never-ending attempt to maintain the myth that I must be a success. I dare not fail or make a mess of things, because if I do, I'm a failure and I immediately feel guilty. It's a horrible cycle of self-condemnation. As soon as I fall flat on my face, I ask, 'Could I have done more? How can I make amends for this mistake? How on earth can I live with myself?' And we heap guilt on ourselves in huge doses. Not only do we feel failures, but we feel guilty failures as well, because we think that maybe we could have done more to prevent it. Guilt and failure together form a lethal combination. The devil pours in tidal waves of condemnation, and rubs in the pain like salt in a wound.

Does the Bible offer a solution? Well, if my failure is due to some identifiable sin, then repentance is the first priority. Not to allow Christ to deal with that sin actually makes me guilty of a much more serious failure – the failure to maintain a close walk with God. Sometimes, when I'm angry with myself about some particular wrongdoing, I may not even want God's forgiveness at that moment, because I'm not yet prepared to forgive myself. But as soon as I admit my sin and failings, God can forgive me and help me. 'Stop wasting your time wallowing in guilt,' he says. 'Receive a fresh cleansing and get on your way for Christ. I know you through and through, and you don't have to prove a thing with me. I love you anyway.'

Self-condemnation and low self-esteem can be combated with the recognition that my significance to God is in no way dependent on my performance. It's all to do with God's unconditional love. Take that marvellous verse with which chapter 8 of the letter to the Romans begins: 'Therefore, there is now no condemnation for those who are in Christ Jesus.' Learn that verse, memorize it, meditate on it, apply it to yourself, and after a while you will have discovered the secret of taking every failure and every defeat, and turning it away from guilt and condemnation, to praise.

You will be able to emulate the seventeenth-century monk Brother Lawrence who, every time he fell and failed, got down on his knees and said, 'Thank you, God, for reminding me of what I'm like apart from you.' Before long you will begin to get into the habit, and it will become a most stimulating experience in the Spirit, getting a whole new mentality and being transformed by the renewing of your mind. However badly you may have failed, God is the God of new beginnings. You have no need to justify yourself. God is your justifier.

Feelings of blame and self-pity

Failure is always painful, but particularly so when it is the result of someone else letting you down. The failure of a marriage can leave deep hurt in a partner who strove with all his or her might to hold the relationship together in the face of persistent adultery or abuse. When you are a victim of someone else's callousness or selfishness, how do you cope with the inevitable emotional fallout?

Blame and self-pity are two common expressions of that fallout. But these are emotions that never bring healing. Research has shown that the more a victim blames another person for some tragedy or failure, the less likely he or she is to cope. Sadly, the insistence on blaming others is an attitude that has grown to epidemic proportions. A graffito scrawled on the wall of a subway in America bore the message: 'Humpty Dumpty was pushed.' That sums up today's attitudes. The question is: should victims forgive and forget, or should they vent their fury, resort to litigation and seek to attribute blame? Certainly, where others were responsible for our painful circumstances, there is every reason to feel aggrieved. There may be a need to seek justice. But if we continue to wallow in self-pity, harbour resentment and blame others, our minds and bodies will suffer.

Many of the tragedies and disasters that befall us do not result in justice being done. And the ongoing fight to ensure that somebody pays can be self-destructive. It's when someone else's sin has gone unpunished that we are least likely to recognize our own sins of bitterness and self-pity. These can fester away within us for years, affecting our minds and bodies. Forgiveness is never easy, but it's absolutely vital if we do not want to be damaged ourselves. Jesus said, 'When you stand praying, if you hold anything against anyone, forgive him, so that your Father in heaven may forgive you your sins' (Mark 11:25). As David Seamands puts it, 'There comes a time in the schedule of God's healing and recovery process when we all have to move beyond hurt to forgiveness, beyond wishful thinking to responsible action, beyond blame to belief. We move into the place where victims can become victorious!'[1]

Avoiding the victim mentality

But what if you are the person responsible for the failure? The ability to come to terms with that reality can sometimes be even harder. In society today, the commonest response is to adopt a victim mentality, or a martyr complex, attributing blame elsewhere. The American comedian Flip Wilson coined the much-quoted line: 'The devil made me do it.' The sketch is highly amusing, but the ironic thing is that the philosophy it portrays ('Don't blame me; it's not my fault') is exactly what the devil wants to promote. And he's been highly successful in today's culture. As a result, all manner of sin, failure and character flaws are put down to 'rage syndrome' or 'alcohol dependence', as well as previously unheard-of phenomena with names like 'emotionally unstable character disorder', or 'chronic truancy syndrome', or 'habitual lateness syndrome'. The excuses become more and more far-fetched.

Modern psychiatry has sometimes contributed to this trend of seeking to attribute the blame elsewhere. As a popular song by Anna Russell humorously expresses it:

I went to my psychiatrist to be psychoanalysed,
To find out why I killed the cat and blacked my husband's eyes.

Once the person is on the couch and the counselling begins, various 'insights' are revealed:

When I was one, my mummy hid my dolly in a trunk,
And so it follows naturally that I'm always drunk.

By the end of the song, the person has reached the following conclusion:

But I am happy now I've learned the lesson this has taught,
That everything I do that's wrong is someone else's fault!

This is the message increasingly conveyed by this widespread philosophy: 'I am not responsible for what has gone wrong.' It's an enormously inviting cop-out. It's a great victory for the devil if he can cause you to find some other source to blame. He doesn't care who takes the rap if it keeps you from emotional wholeness. Sexual abuse, dysfunctional homes, and childhood deprivation have blighted many people's lives. None of us can control circumstances like those. But we *are* responsible for our attitudes and subsequent reactions. Shifting the blame on to God, the devil or other people is one of the best recipes for self-perpetuating failure. Resist with everything you've got any instinctive desire to see yourself as a victim. What happened to you may have been a gross miscarriage of justice, but it need not make you a victim. Being a victim describes who you are, whereas experiencing injustice describes what happened to you. There is a difference. And if your hackles are rising and you are getting upset, keep calm, and read on.

Your identity in Christ

If you are a Christian, you are never a mere victim of circumstances. Otherwise the promise in the Bible that 'in all things God works for the good of those who love him, who have been called according to his purpose' (Romans 8:28), is sheer nonsense. It is God who determines the events of your life, and while such events often don't seem to make much sense to you, God's intention is always to bring good out of them, and never for you to capitulate to the self-pitying role of a victim.

God sees you as someone special, his child (1 John 3:1–2). You are not a failure. That is a description that the Bible never uses of a Christian. It may have been your condition before you came to Christ, and it doesn't help to fool yourself otherwise. The message of the gospel begins with the truth that you have failed to match God's standards. Outside of Christ, we are absolute, total failures. We have to recognize and acknowledge that. But when Jesus becomes our Saviour, and we give our life over to his control, our identity in God's sight fundamentally changes. Jesus is a perfect success, and we are in him. Jesus is perfect victory, and we share that victory.

For a long time I wasted energy trying to prove myself,

defend myself, justify myself, make myself a success in God's eyes. It was a revelation to discover that in Christ I don't have to strain constantly and expend energy in trying not to fail, because I now have unconditional acceptance, a positive power and a sound mind that enables me to share Christ's success and victory. Yes, I may still fail, but there is a huge difference between failing and being a failure. All Christians fail at some stage, but it's no longer true to describe them as failures.

In fact, the same is true for Christians regarding sin. Sinning and being a sinner are two different things. One of the biggest misunderstandings prevalent in the church today concerns our status and identity. We are undoubtedly sinners before we come to Christ, but the Bible nowhere uses that description of someone who has been born again and become a child of God.

Certainly Christians still sin, but our character and identity can no longer be accurately defined by the word 'sinner'. The Bible instead uses the term 'saint' – someone set apart for holiness. I disagree with the *Book of Common Prayer* when it uses the term 'sinners' to refer to Christians.[2] The Bible uses it to describe only those who are unregenerate. Those who belong to Christ have undergone a fundamental change of identity. This is why we are described as a new creation (2 Corinthians 5:17); we have undergone a transformation at the very core of our beings.

And yet Christians often feel themselves to be sinners (and therefore failures) because they have committed some sin, perhaps repeatedly. The failure may indeed have been sin in some form or other, but that does not make them either failures or sinners. When we become Christians we are placed 'in Christ', and since Christ is neither a sinner nor a failure, those are terms that can no longer be applied to us. I still do sin from time to time; I still fail from time to time; but that is no longer symptomatic of who I really am. But if we see ourselves as failures, we will begin to believe that we are failures. And if we believe we are failures, we behave like failures. It's a vicious circle which can only be broken by the renewal of the mind – by focusing and meditating on our true position as children of God.

The fact is, failure is simply an opinion, not an event. Once again, the way we think is what fuels feelings, which in turn spawns behaviour. If those thoughts or perceptions are wrong, then our feelings are not based on truth or reality. And because we associate failure with rejection, it's easy to feel (subconsciously at least) that our acceptance by God is conditional on getting things right. We develop a mental image of a God who always looks down on us with a frown on his face, saying, 'That really wasn't good enough. You must do a lot better than that if you're going to please me.'

The first step to overcoming failure is to recognize that such beliefs are untrue. Wrong feelings are changed by a series of regular daily choices where, little by little, we recognize wrong patterns of thinking, and slowly, with the help of the Spirit, we replace that mindset with a mentality based on truth. Christians can do that better than anyone else in the knowledge that God accepts them just as they are. The Bible stresses again and again that who we are, or what we've done or not done, is not the point. Our acceptance by God is based solely on what Jesus has done on the cross in bearing our sins. 'The cross plus our own achievements,' or 'the cross plus our own efforts' is not the gospel. It doesn't depend on us.

The next step in renewing (or reprogramming) our minds is to focus on Jesus. And remember that what we see in Jesus is a reflection of the Father. Think about the parable of the prodigal son. He was a real failure if ever there was one! And yet the Father came running to welcome him, without condemnation for the past and without conditions for the future. That's the love of God! To quote Adrian Plass, God is 'absolutely crackers about you'!

The more we begin to focus on these truths, the more our wrong thought patterns about failure will slowly begin to change. Bit by bit, I've begun to grasp that God wants me to have the same attitude towards myself that he has. Somebody once challenged me by saying, 'If God accepts you, what right have you to refuse to accept yourself?' If God has transformed our identity in Christ and calls us 'saints', what right have we to think of ourselves as failures?

It's important not to misunderstand at this point. We often get confused about the difference between God accepting us, and God approving of us. God accepts us the way we are, but this doesn't mean that he approves of everything within us. Every parent knows the meaning of that. Parents love their children and accept them the way the are, but that doesn't mean that they always approve of everything they do. That is the way that we can learn to accept ourselves, in spite of our failures and imperfections. When you get that renewed mind through focusing on Jesus, your life is going to be changed, and, painful though failure often is, it becomes the opportunity for God to bring about the growth and maturity that we so desperately need. How is it possible? Well, consider this prayer of Adrian Plass:

On this particular day, I feel a failure.
What am I allowed to wonder, Father?
Am I allowed to wonder why you made it all so difficult?
Even as I say those words the guilt settles.
Perhaps it isn't really difficult at all.
Probably it's me that's difficult.
Probably, because of my background, and my
    temperament,
and my circumstances, it was always going to be difficult
    for me.
But what if that's just a cop-out?
What if I'm kidding myself?
What if, deep inside, I know that my own deliberate doing
    and not doing has always made it difficult?
What if I'm one of those who has been called, but not
    chosen?

In that case it's not difficult – it's impossible.
What if you don't exist at all, and death is a sudden stumble
   into silence?
(Can you let me know if you don't exist, by the way –
   before Friday night, if it's all the same to you.)
There are moments, Father, when it's so easy, so easy that I
   can't remember why it ever seemed so difficult.
Those moments pass – they're valuable – but they pass.
Have you noticed how, when those moments have gone, I
   try to walk away, but I can't?
I think I shall follow you even if you don't exist.
Even if I'm not chosen.
Even if it goes on being difficult . . .
Are you still listening?
I'm sorry to have made a fuss,
It's just that, on this particular day, I feel a failure.
My feet and hands hurt,
And there's this pain in my side.[3]

Notes

1. David Seamands, *If Only . . .* (Scripture Press, 1995), p. 69.
2. 'We sinners do beseech thee to hear us . . .', The Litany, *Book of Common Prayer*.
3. Adrian Plass, *The Unlocking* (Bible Reading Fellowship, 1994), pp. 36–37.

For personal study or group discussion

1. In what ways has God worked for good when you have encountered failure?
2. What is the difference between experiencing injustice and being a victim? Or between failing and being a failure? Can you easily distinguish between sinning and being a sinner? If not, what steps can you take to undergo renewing of your mind?

3. What is the ultimate criterion of success or failure? Is it the criterion you have been living by?

9. Kicking the furniture

The first public talk I ever had to give was on the subject of 'Anger'. It was to a Christian Union at a rather fashionable girls' school in Rhodesia in 1975. I still have the notes I used, condensed straight out of a Christian counselling manual. I have no idea why I was invited, and no idea why I was given that topic. As I stood in front of those high-school girls, not much older than some of them, I think I could have given a more authoritative talk on 'Nerves' than on anger. But I can still remember how, in preparing for that talk, I began to understand a little bit more about this most volatile of emotions, and that perhaps there was a bit more anger within me than I had cared to admit.

What makes you angry? I like to think that I've got a fairly long fuse, but there are certain things that will trigger my anger almost instantaneously. Someone else's bad driving will very quickly get me churned up, and I can understand why we now have a phenomenon known as 'road rage', with regular media reports of drivers who have been beaten up or even murdered by other road-users venting uncontrollable anger. I'm convinced that the nation's annual bill for tranquillizers must have increased in proportion to the ever-growing traffic congestion on our roads.

There are other things that ignite my fuse too. A simple DIY job that goes wrong will be the signal for my wife to retreat upstairs out of my way. She can recognize the signs. And I'm not proud to admit that one dent in our lounge wall was caused by a low-flying missile which was defying all attempts to get it to function as a torch, which was what it was originally designed for. Malfunctioning photocopiers are another invention which often seem to me to serve little purpose other than to raise my blood pressure.

In these kind of instances my anger is short, sharp and very transparent. But when I get angry with people, rather than with objects or circumstances, my anger is scarcely evident at all. It tends to simmer below the surface, in a long, slow-burning resentment, which may only occasionally be evident in the form of some sarcastic comment or cynical remark. I have never had a confrontational personality, and I will rarely lose my cool while in conversation with someone, however provocative they may be. The anger gets internalized, and sometimes I may not even be aware that it is there.

I have learned, however, that neither of these forms of anger is particularly healthy. The Christian counselling manual mentioned above taught me that much. But then the question is: what *is* the best way to handle this emotion? It is probably true to say that out of all the emotions we experience, anger is the one that Christians feel most guilty about. This is usually because the church has very effectively conveyed the message that anger is bad. Certainly it is one of the most difficult emotions to express in a positive, creative way. But much sincere preaching simply condemns anger as being 'unchristian', without providing any clear understanding of the nature of anger or how to deal with it.

9 Kicking the furniture

Christians then experience a great deal of internal conflict, believing that any show of anger is unacceptable and that all their feelings must be suppressed. As a result, committee meetings often spell pain and frustration, and group activities become difficult and unpleasant experiences. Relationships are strained, but by keeping everyone else at an emotional arm's length, the hope is that no-one will get hurt. Well, not severely, anyway.

Recognizing the futility of such a strategy, there was a period when some self-help books stressed the importance of giving vent to one's feelings. We were not encouraged to exercise restraint. It is healthy, we were told, to lash out whenever we feel angry. Parents were led to believe that in order to bring children up correctly, they must allow a child to have temper tantrums whenever it likes. Kicking the furniture, the cat and anything else that gets in the way was said to be therapeutic (for the child, not the cat). Unfortunately, the long-term effects of this behaviour were not immediately appreciated, as the habit-forming results made things very unpleasant for everyone encountering such a volatile person.

Psychologists today emphasize that people should own their feelings in order to take responsibility for their ensuing actions and reactions. The dilemma for many, however, is how to do so effectively. Not everyone has a trained professional who will objectively help them to understand and deal responsibly with their anger. Anger has an uncanny knack of disguising itself in various ways, making it difficult to recognize and confront.

To make things worse, our culture doesn't teach us how to handle anger in a positive way. Not surprisingly, we therefore don't really know what to do with our anger. Is it always wrong? Can we distinguish between the emotion of anger and its expression as hostility and aggression? We are conditioned to believe that it is healthier to express one's anger than to suppress it. But doing that makes other people feel embarrassed and ourselves guilty. Is there not a healthier way of dealing with angry feelings, without either internalizing all our rage or compromising our Christian witness and causing discomfort to others? I believe there is, but we need first to consider the causes of anger.

Anger may have a number of sources, but the most important are frustration, hurt, a conditioned response and the instinct of preservation. For many of us, it is the first two factors that are the most frequent trigger mechanisms.

Dealing with frustration

Frustration builds up when a series of events denies you the achievement or fulfilment that you want. These can be external circumstances, such as when the train you catch to work breaks down and leaves you stranded. Or they can be internal obstacles, such as low self-esteem, feelings of inadequacy, or a long-standing sense of rejection by others. An unfulfilled striving to achieve a measure of self-worth generates a frustration-fed anger that can at times erupt with explosive force.

One reason there are so many frustrated people in society today is that a significant proportion of today's generation grew up accustomed to having their every desire fulfilled in childhood. For many, the benefits of western materialism came too easily. Now they are adults, they discover that their every wish in life is no longer instantly gratified, and they are not used to coping with that. I believe parents act wisely when they teach their children patience, by not continually giving in to a child's every whim and fancy. It will reduce their frustration in later life when they find that other things don't come easily either.

This illustrates how anger caused by frustration can be dealt with by developing a more flexible personality. It pays to discipline ourselves to be adaptable to changing situations. Consider whether perhaps you are being a perfectionist, and therefore intolerant or idealistic in your expectations. Perfectionists often tend to be frustrated people. We are obsessed with wanting to be perfect parents, successful in our careers, accomplished in sport and financially flourishing. We can't handle failure and have great difficulty accepting our fallible humanity. Consciously and deliberately aiming to be flexible will help to minimize our mounting frustration.

James and Nina Rye, in their book *Facing Frustration*,[1] perceptively point out that frustration is often made worse among some Christians by the naïve belief that their faith should exempt them from all blockages to their goals and ambitions. It is only more mature Christians who recognize that God may want to use the experience of thwarted hopes to move them on spiritually and deepen their faith and trust in him.

Dealing with hurt

The second important cause of anger is hurt, which may be physical but is more commonly psychological. This kind of anger can arise when we feel we haven't been treated fairly, or when we are humiliated and our self-worth is undermined. Life is full of potential for hurt and thus can create in us anger at every turn. As Peter Wilkes succinctly puts it: 'Anger is our explosive response to a denial of our significance.'[2]

Many hurts begin in childhood. Bullying at school is an acutely painful reality for many children. They may feel helpless to retaliate and it generates an enormous degree of anger. In the back of their minds they are wanting to tear the other person apart.

When anger such as this is experienced over a long period of time, it creates in us a feeling of simmering indignation which is called resentment. Resentment can breed a whole host of other 'nasties' which can easily take their toll on you physically, mentally and spiritually. Carrying resentment can cause ulcers, high blood pressure and migraines. Personalitywise, such people become unattractive and difficult to relate to. A person holding a grudge frequently becomes sensitive and touchy, suspicious of what others are thinking and saying. It is impossible to be free and happy if we allow our hurts to create unresolved anger in us

every time. Holding someone in the prison of your unforgive-
ness actually imprisons you and not the other person. But how
do you let go?

Some people don't want to let go, because their resentment is
the only weapon they have to try and exact revenge with. It's the
one stick that they can use to beat their tormentors with. This is
despite the fact that it's a totally ineffective and counter-
productive weapon. Jesus told an important parable, aimed at
helping us put our hurts, resentments and desires for revenge in
a proper perspective. It comes in response to Peter's question,
'How many times shall I forgive my brother when he sins
against me?' (Matthew 18:21).

Jesus' story concerns a king who decided to settle accounts
with his servants. One servant had a debt running into millions
of pounds. He pleaded so movingly for more time to pay it back
that the king forgave him and wrote off the entire amount. This
servant, shortly after leaving the king, encountered a fellow
servant who owed him just a few pounds and violently
demanded that the debt be paid. The second servant also pleaded
for mercy, but it was refused. The first servant had him jailed
until the debt was paid. The king was horrified to hear of the
first servant's attitude, and revoked his earlier act of compassion.
Jesus ends the parable with these words:

> In anger his master turned him over to the jailers to be
> tortured, until he should pay back all he owed.
> This is how my heavenly Father will treat each of you
> unless you forgive your brother from your heart (Matthew
> 18:34–35).

The message is clear: I have caused God more hurt than any
other person could ever cause me. Therefore, if God has
forgiven me, what right have I to withhold forgiveness from
those who have hurt me? It is easy to suffer from what has been
called 'hurt myopia', when we invariably see the hurts we cause

others as being insignificant compared to the hurts they cause us. The necessary corrective is to compare the hurts others have caused us with the hurts that we have caused God by our own disobedience and stubbornness. Developing this perspective will help to free us from the prison of resentment. And it is possible only because Christ *first* forgave us.

Admittedly, there is no guarantee that forgiving those who have wronged us will necessarily bring about reconciliation and healed relationships. Forgiveness may be thrown back in our face (God knows what that's like). Our graciousness in forgiving may be construed as patronizing by the recipient, and we may need to think of ways of conveying forgiveness other than by verbally telling them we have done so. Jesus, for example, demonstrated forgiveness to Zacchaeus by making a social visit to his home. But whether our forgiveness is accepted or refused, the Bible still puts the onus on us to take the initiative and forgive. At stake is not only our emotional well-being, but a right relationship with God.

Anger as a conditioned response

This is the next important cause of anger, and it is often learned early in life. We learn how to manipulate people and get our own way by displaying anger. When others give way to this emotional blackmail, the pattern of behaviour is reinforced. The child who throws regular temper tantrums is the obvious example of a conditioned anger response.

The other form of conditioning relates to the company we keep. 'Do not make friends with a hot-tempered man, do not associate with one easily angered, or you may learn his ways and get yourself ensnared' (Proverbs 22:24). The fact is, you become like the people you mix with. If you live in a home where anger is continually being vented, it will become second nature to do likewise. Paul recognized this conditioning effect when he wrote, 'Bad company corrupts good character' (1 Corinthians 15:33). We need to be aware of the insidious conditioning from other people and society around us. Anger can be a response that is easily learned by bad example.

Anger as instinctive protection

Anger is one of the primary emotions, present right from birth. If you withhold milk from a baby, you will trigger this instinctive rage response which is designed to be part of our survival make-up. While it may be very rare today to need anger for survival, the purpose of this type of anger is to provide the courage and motivation to defend ourselves and overcome any threatening obstacles. Used constructively, this is a healthy form of anger. It can actually help us function better both physically and mentally.

Righteous anger

In some situations, guided by reason and self-control, anger can be the right response. The Bible certainly envisages that there will be circumstances where anger is legitimate. Paul's words 'In your anger do not sin' (Ephesians 4:26) deal the deathblow to the idea that Christians must all be doormats, passive individuals who never get angry. A Christian can and should get angry. After all, God does. Like God, however, we must ensure that we get angry over the right issues.

We must also be careful in the way such anger is exercised. What Paul is saying is not that the feeling of anger itself is wrong, but that anger has the potential for leading us into sin. There is no blanket condemnation of anger as an inherently sinful emotion. It is the wrong actions that tend to arise out of such anger that are condemned. Feelings are legitimate. What we *do* with our feelings is where we run the risk of going wrong.

The truth is, we are at our most dangerous when we are 'righteously angry', because it's then that we are least conscious of our own sin. Do you know who we tend to be most angry with? It's people who act like us. We get angry with people who are doing the sorts of thing that subconsciously we still struggle with. Have you ever wanted to wipe out somebody, in the belief that you're doing the world a favour? In reality, your anger may be directed not so much at purging the world of evil, but because you don't want your nice, happy lifestyle to be inconvenienced by their wrongdoing. It upsets your smooth, tranquil existence. And the danger of righteous anger is that we can end up thinking we're more righteous than God, whereas in fact we haven't dealt with our own sin within.

If our anger is going to remain righteous, therefore, our motives must be laid bare before the Holy Spirit. Otherwise we can end up as Christian vigilantes, fighting raging battles against injustice. Righteous anger is least contaminated when it's directed at injustice done to others. If our own reputation, status or pride is involved, we will have reason to examine our motivation with suspicion.

Not only can our righteous anger be a clever device to blind us to similar tendencies within ourselves, it can be a means of justifying revenge. When we have been personally hurt or treated unjustly, our human nature always wants to even the score. This is why Paul said:

> Do not repay anyone evil for evil. Be careful to do what is right in the eyes of everybody. If it is possible, as far as it depends on you, live at peace with everyone. Do not take revenge, my friends, but leave room for God's wrath, for it is written: 'It is mine to avenge; I will repay,' says the Lord (Romans 12:17–19).

Secondly, our anger must not only be righteous, it must also be controlled. However righteous the cause, anger becomes sinful when it's not subject to reason or restraint. The mind must be in charge of the emotions. Anger can easily take over so that we lose control of ourselves.

Thirdly, there must be no hatred, malice or resentment. Consider the way in which Jesus responded to the insults and injustices meted out to him: 'When they hurled their insults at him, he did not retaliate; when he suffered, he made no threats. Instead, he entrusted himself to him who judges justly' (1 Peter 2:23).

The anger of God

Mention of God's judgment leads us to consider the nature of God's anger. 'The wrath of God' is a phrase that occurs quite regularly in the Bible. And if God is good and holy, this is perhaps the clearest example of all that anger should not always be considered wrong. Sadly, this term 'the wrath of God' has been terribly misunderstood. Just as the human usage of the word 'love' frequently falls far short of the quality of love we attribute to God, so our understanding of 'wrath' can be quite misleading. We cannot assume that the anger of God is exactly like our anger, which is prone to containing personal malice, or vindictiveness, or revenge. God is not bad-tempered; he does not vent his irritation by trying to get his own back on fallible human beings. It is wrong to see anger as the opposite of love. Sometimes anger is an expression of love.

God's anger is the personal reaction of his holy character to the presence or practice of sin. His holiness demands that he cannot remain indifferent. And that anger is something that he shows. God does not bottle up his anger within himself. It is an active thing, which will have an effect on people and events. Sometimes that anger is shown over a long period of time as a slow process. At other times the Bible talks of a sudden crisis, a 'day of wrath', when his anger is expressed quickly and unexpectedly.

The first kind of anger is what God is demonstrating in our world now. He responds to the intransigence of human sin and rebellion by withdrawing the restraining power of his Holy Spirit. That is an expression of his anger and, in my view, it explains the ever-increasing downhill slide in human behaviour in the present day. God in his anger has released the brakes on society. The moral rottenness, greed and immorality, so graphically described at the end of Romans 1, are not only the cause of God's anger, but also, startlingly, the result of it. These consequences are more obvious in some cultures and societies than others, but they are clear indications of God's anger. The other kind of anger – the sudden kind – God will show in the future on judgment day, the dramatic and decisive intervention into human history which is outlined on more than one occasion in the Bible.

Perhaps the clearest picture of God's holy anger can be seen in the life of Jesus. When Jesus became angry, he did so in response to the stubbornness, sin and unbelief he encountered in people. When religious people got upset when he healed on the Sabbath, 'He looked round at them in anger and, deeply distressed at their stubborn hearts, said to the man, "Stretch out your hand." He stretched it out, and his hand was completely restored' (Mark 3:5). Notice how his anger was entirely without selfish motives. There was no desire for revenge, or need to retaliate against those who hurt him. He was responding to a situation where an innocent man's need and disability were being used as a political and religious football. His anger was essentially on behalf of others.

This will be a useful principle for us as we now consider how to direct our anger in the right way and to the right causes.

Notes

1. James and Nina Rye, *Facing Frustration* (Crossway Books, 1997), p. 15.
2. Peter Wilkes, *Mastering the Dragons of the Soul* (IVP, 1987), p. 34.

10. Dealing with anger

It is not the fact that people get angry that causes so many problems in society. It is the fact that people get angry over the wrong issues, and from the wrong stimuli. The desperate need we face is how to retrain this emotion, and channel it in constructive ways. This may explain why so many businesses and organizations are running courses on the rare quality of 'assertiveness'. The majority of people are either passive or aggressive in personality, and both of these characteristics breed anger. Passive behaviour frequently results in internalized anger when other people ride roughshod over us and we don't stand up to that. Aggressive behaviour encourages outward expressions of anger which lose us friendships and leave us feeling embarrassed and ashamed of our lack of control.

Assertiveness, on the other hand, avoids both passivity and aggression. It is the polite and courteous firmness that often defuses potential anger from both ends of the spectrum. Being resolute by respectfully expressing your feelings or opinions, while at the same time acknowledging the feelings and opinions of others, is a very constructive way of avoiding conflict. It takes courage to be firm, but when you are, you walk away from the situation feeling good about yourself, rather than angry for giving in, or for blowing your top. The need for developing assertiveness is being recognized by the growing number of courses being offered to help people develop such skills, and Christians shouldn't devalue their potential usefulness.

Various forms of anger, of course, need addressing in specific ways. Numerous methods have been promoted to try and help people deal with their anger, but, it has to be said, most fall short of the biblical solution. Let's consider a few of the common ones.

Repression

One unconscious strategy that many people adopt is to repress their anger, ignoring its presence. The easiest option is to bury it and not even admit that it's there. Have you ever been around a seemingly passive person, and yet sensed that they were potentially dangerous? They may have seemed mild, and even docile, and yet you were aware that beneath that passivity there was a ticking bomb. Perhaps it's fear of the intensity of rage that could come out if they ever let themselves feel their feelings that brings about this repression.

But holding your anger beneath the surface, trying to force it out of your conscious awareness, is always harmful. The energy produced by anger doesn't just spontaneously dissipate. If it is repressed, it will simply seek another outlet. I recently counselled a woman whose husband walked out on her fifteen years ago for another woman. She sincerely believed that she was not an angry person. She believed anger was an unacceptable emotion, and she sought to maintain a calm and serene exterior. She was, however, suffering from arthritis and depression and finding life hard to cope with. It took some time before she could bring herself to admit that she had been gaining pleasure from the thought of inflicting torture on her ex-husband's lover by pulling out her fingernails one by one. Once she realized her anger and was able to allow Christ to deal with it, her arthritis and depression improved quite markedly, and she felt able to face the future for the first time for years.

I have counselled all manner of people whose buried anger has taken its toll on them physically, with high blood pressure, headaches, gastric ulcers, colitis and other disorders. Repressed anger can also result in chronic mental depression, and is therefore damaging psychologically as well as physically.

Suppression

If repression is the *unconscious* denial of one's anger, an alternative, but equally unproductive, way of dealing with anger is *consciously* to hide, or suppress, one's feelings. In this case, a person will be aware of anger, but will choose to hold it in, and conceal his or her feelings from those who have caused it. In some situations this may be healthy and wise, but it can also be a recipe for misery. Francis is, by all outward appearances, a quiet and placid person. But when we met he poured out a torrent of emotional pain. There was a huge well of pent-up anger within, relating to abuse and injustice he had experienced over many years in his workplace. He was like a pressure-cooker that was bursting. He suffered chronic neck and shoulder pain, but his doctor said that he couldn't help other than by providing painkillers. Francis still spends long hours alone, brooding. He rarely communicates with anybody. He acknowledges that the emotional boil needs to be lanced and the poison drawn from his mind, but as far as I'm aware, he hasn't been able to face that challenge yet.

The other danger is that suppression frequently results in 'scapegoating', or displaced anger. This is the tendency to take anger that has been generated in one place and dump it in another. It is more commonly known as the 'kick the cat syndrome'. The real source of the anger never receives that anger response. It is transferred to a much 'safer' person or object.

Your long-suffering marriage partner, children or loved ones bear the brunt when your employer has upset you. It may make you feel better to get rid of your anger this way, but it won't do much for good relationships at home.

I recently watched a television documentary which filmed scores of angry passengers dumping their wrath on the check-in clerk at an airport, because their flight was delayed by a strike of air-traffic controllers. In watching this display of uncontrolled abuse, I wondered whether these passengers would have spoken the same way to the air-traffic controllers had they had the opportunity. Check-in clerks, and others who deal with the public, trained as they are to be unfailingly courteous and polite, become an easy target. No wonder some groups of employees in such positions have been campaigning for protective screens on their counters. And yet these people themselves are rarely the source of the anger. They are simply the victims of scapegoating.

Expression

Well-meaning friends may recommend that the best method of dealing with your anger is simply to give vent to it, to unload all your feelings on the hapless offender, no matter what or who is involved. This approach is based on the belief that it is emotionally and physically harmful to try to internalize a feeling of such intensity. 'When people upset you, don't bottle it up. Get it out of your system,' is today's commonly held opinion.

Simon Peter adopted this impulsive policy in slicing off the ear of Caiaphas' servant when Jesus was arrested in the Garden of Gethsemane (John 18:10). Human 'nuclear explosions' such as this can certainly bring results, but the fallout is obvious. If you exercise the freedom to lose your temper, why shouldn't your antagonist do likewise? The person who bites is likely to get bitten back. What's worse is that however emotionally satisfying it may seem to get everything off your chest and let off steam, it neither removes the cause of the anger nor drains away the angry feelings.

My understanding of the Bible's teaching is that there is something wrong with all these approaches. God's answer is one which requires confession.

Confession

The solution is not to pray for your anger to be eradicated or taken away from you. It is better to pray that your anger will be rechannelled towards those things that make God angry. The emotion of anger may be inevitable, but it is vital to minimize its potential for sin. This means anger must not remain unresolved. The Bible says, 'Do not let the sun go down while you are still angry' (Ephesians 4:26). There's good sense in observing that time limit.

To begin with, you need to acknowledge the fact that you are angry – to yourself, to God and, if appropriate, to the person involved. But unload your feelings on God, not on the other person. Every now and again in the Bible you stumble across some prayers which seem to contain astonishing sentiments by the standards of our civilized, sanitized minds. In Psalm 109, David prays for all manner of curses and retribution on those who have maligned him and plotted evil against him. David's sentiments may not have been 100% Christian, but he was tackling his anger more constructively by taking it to God than by venting it on those who had upset him.

Sometimes it's no longer possible to vent one's anger on the offender, because the event took place many years ago. Here it's important to be aware that the anger we feel is not something accumulated from the past. Anger occurs only in the here and now. This is the case with all feelings and emotions. They exist only in the present. I cannot be experiencing yesterday's anger today. The truth is, rather, that yesterday's memory of some incident has the ability to recreate anger within me today.

This has important implications for how we deal with our anger. Essentially, it is the *power* of our memories that incites anger, and it is this that must be tackled – not by some trite and simplistic 'Forgive and forget' philosophy, but by breaking the power of those memories.

If the memories are still generating anger today, then it may be advantageous to receive ministry for their healing. Through prayer, the Holy Spirit can take us back in our imaginations to the time of the actual experience, and Jesus then accompanies us through the painful memory, in such a way that his love, his comfort, his compassion, his forgiveness and his reassuring presence begin to penetrate through the 'pain barrier'. This ministry is not an attempt to rewrite history, but it allows Jesus to minister to us in a conscious way in the manner we needed at the time of the incident. The result is that the intense emotional sting is drawn, and the anger or hurt can be released to him in a positive way so that the grip such a memory has on us today can be broken.

This is because Christ transcends all of time. The Bible speaks of him being the same yesterday, today and for ever (Hebrews 13:8). Time is the finite concept by which you and I experience reality. But God lives within no such restrictions, and he is able to perform emotional surgery on the memories that are so painful. But let me emphasize that this is no magical gimmick. It's grace. Just as God can break the chains of past sin in our lives, so he can break the chains of past memories. There's nothing unbiblical about unlocking sensitive memories and releasing resentment, hurt and anger to the love and healing power of Christ.

You will need to pray with an experienced person in whom you have complete trust and confidence in a 'safe' environment. It can be very traumatic, and if embarked upon without sufficient care, even counter-productive. But, gently and sensitively exercised, such ministry can bring very significant release. The healing may come quickly, or it may take several weeks. But God will answer the prayer of faith.

The process is never complete, however, without forgiveness. Of course, an angry person can easily find God's demand to forgive even more infuriating. But without forgiveness, the battle with anger will never be fully won. Yet it's not a step that comes easily. Where people have experienced rejection, injustice, abuse and other equally damaging treatment from other people, anger is an almost inevitable result. In such situations we think that if we dispense instant forgiveness, that automatically trivializes the incident. It conveys the message that it was something unimportant, and we refuse to allow that to be the case. Of course, something so hurtful or damaging is important. But then, how is real forgiveness ever possible?

Wise counsellors have recognized that forgiveness often needs to be a process, rather than a one-off event. Perhaps that process has to start with a willingness to give up thoughts of revenge. The Bible's message on this is unambiguous: 'Do not repay anyone evil for evil' (Romans 12:17). If you cannot yet bring yourself to forgive, then do at least start to pray for the person you are so angry with. In the Sermon on the Mount, Jesus taught that we should pray for those who persecute us (Matthew 5:44). We may wish to pray that they would repent, or that they would have an encounter with Christ, but, assuming we don't pray curses and damnation upon them, whatever we pray will be a stepping-stone towards forgiveness. I have found this to be one of the most constructive ways of dealing with anger. It is hard to pray sincerely for someone for any length of time without finding yourself moving down the path of forgiveness.

Often, forgiveness suddenly becomes possible when healing prayer for the hurting memories has taken place. If Jesus has stepped into that memory and brought healing, anger tends to lose its cutting edge. Nevertheless, emotions can be resurrected by any incident that reminds us of the original cause. Then forgiveness may need to be repeated again and again. Just as bereavement brings recurring waves of grief, we can experience recurring waves of anger from past events. That is not unusual. But we then need to take these back to God honestly and ask him to deal with them.

Sometimes, however, we may feel this process to be compli-
cated because the person we are angry with is God himself! The
guilt that goes with that recognition only intensifies the anguish.
Rather than admit this, we sometimes find a substitute object for
our anger. But being angry with God is not the unforgiveable sin.
It is often the natural reaction of a finite mind wondering why an
omnipotent God permitted some personally devastating experience to happen. But God doesn't mind! Job got angry with God
(see Job 10), and God had broad enough shoulders to take it,
and the infinite love not to be offended. So don't ever be afraid
to admit the fact to God if you feel angry with him.

Anger such as this can be a reaction to love that is seemingly
withheld or denied. When the mind and the intellect sense a
contradiction between the reality of God's love and the reality of
some incomprehensible experience, it's easy to conclude that
God has let us down, and his love is not adequate or personal.
The solution lies in focusing afresh on the truth of God's Word,
so that our minds absorb his unconditional love, and the void is
filled and the hurts healed. The results may not be instant-
aneous; it took Job some considerable time before God's Word
penetrated through his anger and self-pity. The truths of God
absorbed into the mind and heart always act as a disinfectant,
however, dealing with the festering infections of our sinfulness.
Then, with the strength that he supplies, the space in our minds
that was occupied by anger can begin to be occupied by love.
And as Eddie Askew says in his poem, that's a space that may
take some filling:

> Lord, there are times when I feel so angry!
> Some word said, some action
> which makes me feel hurt or slighted.
> And I respond instinctively.
> I lash out in blind rage.
> I want to hurt, I want to crush him,
> to see him speechless, humiliated.

The harsh words, the sarcasm I label 'humour',
out beyond recall before I know it.
Sometimes I say nothing.
But the anger is still there,
the words bouncing around my mind
in a nuclear explosion of rancour.
My body aches with tension, taut with grievance.
And I try to hide it, Lord.
Somehow it seems wrong to admit it, to confess
 my anger.
I pretend it isn't there,
I push it down into that black hole inside me
where it seethes and bubbles
and transforms into bitterness.
And it poisons my life.

They made you angry, Lord.
The Pharisees with their hypocrisy.
The traders bringing their dishonesty into the temple.
There's a place for it when it's not selfish.
But my anger isn't 'righteous'. Far from it.
Lord, I don't want it like that.
I want to be free.
I want to be in control, to weigh my words.
I want to think before I speak,
(isn't it easy to say, Lord?),
to understand before I act.
And if I understood, really understood,
maybe I wouldn't be angry at all.
Lord I've tried. And tried again.
It's time I asked you.
I think of you before Pilate, and Herod, not opening
 your mouth.
I think of your cross.
No anger – just words of forgiveness – even then.

10 Dealing with anger

Lord, take my anger. Nail it to your cross.
And fill the space it leaves with your love.
It's a big space. It will take some filling.[1]

Note

1. Eddie Askew, *A Silence and a Shouting* (The Leprosy Mission, 1993), p. 31.

For personal study or group discussion

1. Do you feel that it is always unchristian to get angry? If so, why?
2. What kind of situation prompts you to feel angry inside and yet unable to express that anger? Is there perhaps an appropriate way of expressing your feelings?
3. What situations or experiences have prompted you to feel angry during recent weeks? How can you test whether the anger that you feel is 'righteous' or not? Make a list of the steps you need to take to handle that anger more constructively.

11. The pall of depression

Britain today consumes more antidepressants than antibiotics. Nearly three million men and women – or 5% of the British population – are diagnosed as suffering from some form of depression (and others suffer without seeking medical help). That's an indication of how widespread a problem depression has become in a country obsessed with the 'feel-good factor'. I guess more volumes have been written in recent years on how to overcome depression than on any other emotion. The trouble is, depressed people have neither the concentration nor the motivation to read screeds of learned opinions. So I'm very conscious that lengthy analysis and spiritually intense prescriptions won't help. In fact, if you are depressed, you might find it easier to read this chapter in small chunks, rather than attempting to wade your way through in one sitting. Or perhaps a friend or partner could read the chapter and then discuss those bits of it that might be helpful to you. With this in mind, part of the chapter is addressed to those who are experiencing depression, and part is directed to those who

11 The pall of depression

may be supporting and seeking to help someone who is depressed.

For the first time in my life, I experienced depression six years ago. I didn't recognize it at the time, because it's a condition that is sometimes masked by a number of disguises. Everybody will know people who say, 'I feel so depressed, so miserable,' and that seems to have become a way of life with them. But feeling miserable is far too generalized a definition of depression. Actually, there is a whole range of symptoms that people complain of. Many of these are experienced quite normally and naturally at different times of life and are totally unrelated to depression.

You feel as if life has kicked the stuffing out of you. The things that motivated you to get out of bed every morning are suddenly of no interest. A feeling of emptiness is very common – of not mattering and not counting: 'Nobody cares about me, nobody wants me.' There is also lethargy, when you feel you just can't be bothered with anything; a change in sleeping habits; an inability to concentrate or make decisions. Other symptoms include irritability, the loss of pleasure, low moods, changes in weight (either by stopping eating or by overeating); a feeling of inappropriate guilt – feeling that you're responsible for something that actually wasn't your fault. All these things happen to us at various stages of life, but the combination of many of them happening together points to a diagnosis of depression.

Depression is recognized by the medical profession not simply as an emotional problem, but also as a physical problem, a chemical imbalance. It is a persistent condition; if what you experience comes and goes, it may not be what the medical profession calls depression. And the doctor's first strategy when encountering depression will be to ensure that the cause isn't something physical, like anaemia or abnormal thyroid function. But whatever the source of the problem, depression is an enormous trial for the sufferer. It's compounded by the confusion which asks, 'Why am I so tired? Why can't I function normally? Why am I not getting better when I have faith and am doing all the things the doctor told me to?'

My own encounter with depression, following a post-viral syndrome, entailed flattened emotions, sudden energy loss, anxiety, bouts of crying for no accountable reason and a loss of interest in the things that normally motivate me. I functioned mechanically, but even simple things seemed demanding and stressful. I lost confidence in my ability to do even those things I was good at. Nevertheless, I would not have described myself simply in terms of feeling miserable.

This is one of the surprising features of depression. It often manifests itself not as an excessively negative emotion, but as no emotion at all. Lethargy rather than misery can be the dominant symptom. The mind seems to shut down and engage neutral gear. It becomes difficult not only to feel happy about something, but also to feel very sad either. This is not uncommonly because the mind is subconsciously trying to avoid dealing with an emotional trauma that it feels unable to cope with. It may be the prospect of redundancy, poor health or disability. Or it may be the result of financial problems, abortion, bereavement, divorce, broken relationships or a betrayal of trust, perhaps from many years previously.

Peter had lived with depression for many years when I first met him. He was in his seventies, and constantly felt inadequate and experienced deep melancholia. He felt guilty for his lack of ambition and motivation, and berated himself for not being more productive. His life was plagued by unreasonable fears, and he repeatedly became tense when thinking about any unpleasant prospects that had to be faced. He was a gentle man who loved God deeply, but further investigation revealed that his mother had died when he was aged seven, and he had grown up with a father who showed very little love or affection. What's more, he had never really grieved over his mother's death. He had been protected from the sorrow by his older brothers and sister, and was given no explanation for the suddenness of her death. Later in life, he had felt acute despair when his fiancée broke off their engagement, but he knew of no way in which he could release the emotional pain. Eventually he had a nervous breakdown, and was told by a psychiatrist that he was seeking a substitute mother figure.

But many years later all those emotions were still bottled up within him and, not knowing how to cope with them, his mind had flattened everything with an all-pervading depression. Try as he might, he found it very hard to tap into the cauldron of grief, anger, guilt and despair within him. But over many months the Holy Spirit very gently led him through various stages of emotional release, and, following each milestone, he found the depression progressively losing its grip.

Of course, depression can have many other causes as well. It is not helpful to categorize all depressions as being spiritual or emotional in origin. But whatever the cause, what makes the problem worse for many Christians is that the very experience of depression is the opposite of what they expect the Christian life to be. They have been fooled into thinking that the Christian life is supposed to be one long 'high'. Surely I'm supposed to be happy all the time, and constantly praising God from the moment my feet hit the floor in the morning?

The reality is that depression brings a feeling of despair, whereas knowing Christ is supposed to give us hope for the future. Why would I be feeling despair when I'm a Christian and I should be experiencing joy? It also gives a feeling of inappropriate guilt, and yet as a Christian I should be experiencing forgiveness. Similarly, depression gives rise to a feeling of low esteem – 'I don't matter.' But as a Christian, of all people, I should know that I am precious in God's sight. He sent his Son for me. If I'm that precious, why should I feel so awful? Why should I feel that I don't matter to anybody? Although I may know in my head that God loves me, there is no conscious experience of that in my heart.

There is no simple explanation which resolves all these paradoxes. But then there's something very incongruous in Paul's summary of what God taught him: 'My grace is sufficient for you, for my power is made perfect in weakness' (2 Corinthians 12:9). That doesn't make depression any easier to embrace. But the reality is that when we are at our least capable, we can hold on to the fact that such importance allows greater opportunity for God's grace to operate.

It is not a sign of spiritual failure to feel depressed. Being born again, filled with the Spirit, and 'washed in the blood' does not affect your body chemistry, your temperament, or the way in which your glands function. To say that no Christian should ever suffer from depression is as ridiculous as saying that no Christian should ever suffer from flu.

Depression is not . . .

Depression may be a many-headed monster, but not every feeling of gloom or despondency is indicative of this condition. It's important to distinguish depression from ordinary unhappiness that is the lot of any human being and is the result of circumstances around us that may change or get better. Mourning is the most typical example of that. Mourning is a very severe process that we all have to go through to some degree when we lose someone (or something) dear to us. It can't really be called depression unless it becomes protracted and doesn't make any progress. Clearly, the loss of someone near to you can provoke an episode of depression. But being unhappy and feeling miserable and not sleeping after the loss of a loved one is a normal and temporary stage.

Similarly, conviction of wrongdoing (or sin) is not the same as depression, although it may masquerade as such. On many occasions I have had to help people complaining of depression, who were actually experiencing an appropriate sense of guilt.

In Africa I once had a young woman in my congregation who seemed persistently depressed. Life constantly seemed to be on top of her. She kept telling me, 'I'm wicked. I'm evil.' With gentle probing, I eventually uncovered the reason for her depression: she was a lonely person living far from her home, and, against all her principles, she was sleeping with a boyfriend, who was merely using her. While she recognized that she was doing wrong, she was reluctant to repent, and not surprisingly felt miserable.

When you are not living in a right relationship with God, you're not going to feel better until you've sought forgiveness and confessed what's wrong. In those circumstances, it would be wrong to go to a doctor or psychiatrist and try to get some tablets to make you feel better. Appropriate guilt is different from depression, even if some of the symptoms appear similar. The two must not be confused.

Depression also differs from the normal despondency that people experience when something has gone wrong. Normally, such people will bounce back sooner or later, depending on their resilience. This is because they still have a hope that things will improve; tomorrow will be better. One of the distinctive symptoms of depression is lack of hope. A person suffering from depression doesn't bounce back. Mild depression or normal despondency will usually resolve itself within the space of two or three weeks, but any depression which persists longer than a month needs professional intervention, particularly if there appears to be no immediately discernible cause. Such a person needs help, whether the symptoms are mild or severe. Mild symptoms that are not dealt with run the danger of becoming severe.

Depressed people will often speak of taking radical measures such as resigning from their job, or leaving their spouse, feeling that they are incapable and that they're letting everybody down. They feel that the present is unbearable, but the future looks even worse. There is no perceived prospect of things getting better, no way out. Even suicide can seem a totally logical step for a severely depressed person. The struggle to go on living seems pointless. If you know someone in that state, it is unwise to ignore comments made about 'ending it all', or any other allusions to suicide. Neither is it wise to try to argue them out of such a viewpoint. A depressed person's mind does not readily respond to reason or even to scriptural exhortations. Such a person needs medical treatment and ongoing, supportive friendship. It is important to be non-judgmental, remembering that the condition is caused by illness and not by sin, obstinate pessimism, or lack of faith. For them, the light at the end of the tunnel is non-existent.

How can you help yourself?

How can that light be switched back on again? Realistically, it needs to be said that there is very little that depressed people can do for themselves. No amount of willpower or spiritual exercises can get them out of depression. Books which advocate thinking more positively, praying more fervently, rebuking demons or memorizing Scripture verses rarely help. People suffering from chronic depression are in no position to help themselves. They simply lack the mental and physical resources to do so.

I have frequently counselled depressed people who have been told by others to 'praise God regardless'. This is wonderfully sound advice to someone undergoing the typical setbacks of everyday life, but it is an oppressive load to ask depressed people to shoulder. They don't possess the mental strength consciously to contradict their present feelings. They probably feel much more like calling God every name in the book. Fair enough. God's got broad enough shoulders to take it, and he's not going to be offended by it.

When you read the Psalms you discover that the writers were transparently honest to God about their feelings. They accused him of forgetting them (Psalms 13 and 42), deserting them (Psalm 22), rejecting them (Psalms 44, 60 and 74) and ignoring them (Psalms 28 and 55). Clearly, they had no qualms about letting off steam to God. It's better to dump all your depression and despair on God than not to pray at all. He knows how you feel anyway, so you're not fooling him.

An important factor in survival for a depressed person is being able to separate the way you feel from what you do. It may seem impossible to think positive thoughts that are true and right (Philippians 4:8), but it is sometimes still possible to believe what is true and do what is right, despite the way you feel. While you may feel utterly unable to combat the feelings, it helps if you recognize that those feelings don't necessarily reflect reality. It will still be easier to act out those subjective emotions. But a willingness to persevere in your marriage relationship and in your church attendance (to mention but two examples), because that is objectively right, will be of benefit even when your feelings are shouting differently. You may not succeed all the time, but the attempt at least to *do* the right thing often provides a platform of resistance which prevents a total disintegration of self-esteem and self-restraint.

What others can do

It may not sound very helpful to say that when you are clinically depressed (rather than merely feeling 'down'), there is virtually nothing you can do to help yourself. But you can allow others to help you. A good doctor or professional counsellor is the first essential, and a supportive friend or relative will usually be willing to help in finding one for you if need be. A dislike of taking tablets is not an acceptable excuse! Another common obstacle among some Christians can be a deep-seated fear and mistrust of medical and psychiatric support when faced with depression. It's seen as an admission that their faith has failed. They want to rely on God, not on scientists. It's difficult for some Christians to rely on a chemical means of helping their emotions, when they believe they should be trusting in God.

In fact, there is no contradiction here. I don't see any difficulty in trusting God for my daily needs and the food that

I eat, and still going to the supermarket to buy it. I don't have a problem with supermarkets being the means of providing for my need. I see it as the way in which God's provision is made accessible in my circumstances. And I do believe that we need to accept that medicine has something to offer.

It is no sin to be on antidepressants. And of course, drugs are not the only option. One of the things that doctors have learned over the past few years is that you don't just have to use tablets to make people better when they have depression. It is a chemical problem, but it's been noticed that in moderate depression, people get well just as often and just as quickly if they are taught to think differently about themselves and recognize their faulty thought patterns. (Do you, for example, tend to see everything in black and white? Is there any room for flexibility in what you think? Maybe you set unrealistic expectations for yourself, or make mountains out of molehills.) This strategy, known as cognitive therapy, is a very popular way of dealing with mild to moderate depression nowadays, when there isn't a suicidal risk.[1] A blanket dismissal of these types of medical help is actually misguided, and Christians need feel no embarrassment in receiving such help.

I said that depressed people also need a supportive friend or relative. This is not the kind of 'help' where a well-meaning Christian tells them that God will use this experience for their ultimate good (which he will); or attempts to get them to cheer up and look on the bright side; or prescribes well-meaning spiritual remedies. All such attempts at help are profoundly irritating to depressed people. They need a friend who will support them and love them without being intrusive, prescriptive or invading their personal space.

In writing about his road to recovery, a man called Warren once stated:

During those years of suffering I needed the care and support of friends who were there for the long haul. I simply needed to be loved as Jesus loved. I didn't need to be condemned nor judged nor ignored, but shown compassion, understanding and huge amounts of patience. I needed to be encouraged to think positively, to be reminded that I did have some value and that, in God's time, I was going to be restored. The visit, the phone call, the note, the hand on the shoulder can all play a part in the restoration process.[2]

As with all emotions, depression responds to whatever thoughts are occupying the mind. With other emotions like anger and fear, it's possible consciously to realign one's thinking with God's truth. The solution there lies in refocusing on what you know about God, rather than on your negative feelings. But with depression this can be utterly beyond your capability. You lack the inner drive and mental energy to try consciously to counter the way you feel. No person in depression has the inner drive to tackle his or her own need.

Here's why it's important for someone else to feed the person's weakened mind in a way that doesn't demand any mental energy. If you are the supportive spouse or friend, don't try to encourage the depressed person to praise God in all circumstances, as some well-meaning Christian counsellors suggest. Rather, try reading your friend some of the Psalms – not in big, indigestible doses, but in short and regular snippets. They can be psalms of praise; equally, they can be psalms of anguish and pain.

Music is another helpful way to feed a depressed mind. King Saul discovered that centuries ago. The Old Testament records show he would have David play the harp for him when, commentators believe, he was overcome with depression (1 Samuel 16:14–23). Music can be deeply moving – even to someone like me, whose knowledge and appreciation of the finer points of music are almost non-existent. Listening to some stirring song or piece of music doesn't require any great expenditure of energy, and on many occasions has proved enormously beneficial to me. And don't think that such music must inevitably be something spiritual. Whether secular or sacred, music has an uncanny ability to tap into the emotions and touch a wounded spirit.

God has created us in such a way that our minds can respond to things other than words, logic and reason. When your mind shuts down in these areas, allow God to refresh it from some other source. Music is only one option. More than once I have experienced a sense of returning peace and hope when I've got alone with God in the vast expanse of the African bush, or stood gazing at the waves of the Indian Ocean pounding the coastline. Consider Elijah. This unflinching, unflappable prophet plummeted to the depths of depression following his triumphant but enormously stressful contest with the prophets of Baal. Full of fear and weariness, he fled alone into the desert (1 Kings 19:3–4).

Sometimes it can be plain silly to isolate yourself when you're depressed. It shuts you off from every available human source of help. At other times, it can be helpful to let God meet with you in the vastness of nature. Alone on Mount Horeb, Elijah encountered the powerful forces of nature – earthquakes, wind and fire – following which, God's still, gentle whisper helped him to regain his perspective.

In the next chapter we shall look at how God's recovery plan worked for Elijah, and what hope we can draw from that for ourselves.

Notes

1. A useful book dealing with this in more detail, but which is easy reading, is Susan Tanner and Jillian Ball, *Beating the Blues: A Self-Help Approach to Overcoming Depression* (Doubleday, Moorebank), 1991.
2. 'Warren's story', *The Briefing*, 22 September 1997, p. 10.

12. God's recovery plan

It's interesting to see the way God dealt with Elijah's depression. He began by refusing to answer Elijah's prayer. Elijah prayed that he might die. 'I have had enough, LORD. Take my life; I am no better than my ancestors' (1 Kings 19:4). And God in his mercy ignored that prayer. When we are depressed we commonly ask for the wrong things, and God will just not answer those prayers. Not surprisingly, that may only intensify our depression. 'Not even God is listening to me now.' It isn't that. He just doesn't want to answer that kind of prayer. So there was no response.

God's strategy for helping Elijah is very practical. First of all, he sends an angel with a meal, and lets him have a good sleep. (When you are depressed, the two things that are almost invariably affected straight away are your eating and sleeping habits.) It's as though God told the angel, 'Go and cook a meal for Elijah.' God could have rebuked his despairing prophet. He could have pensioned him off, and replaced him with someone who was less war-weary. He could have reminded Elijah of umpteen spiritual truths which had clearly slipped his mind. But no. Elijah's problem of depression was initially tackled physically, with a simple act of caring.

A lady in my congregation baked me a chocolate cake this week. That little gesture served not only to put calories into my body, but encouragement into my spirit. Now make no mistake, Elijah needed the calories. He had just run 18 miles, which was no mean distance for a middle-aged man, and he'd had no food for a long time. He had been fasting as well as praying. So he was physically exhausted. He needed to rest and recover his strength. Instead of that, he journeyed another 90 miles south to Beersheba. It doesn't surprise me that he collapsed in a state of utter depression, feeling suicidal. Many depressed people I encounter are perfectionists suffering from burnout, having been busy seven days a week. And what the angel provided for Elijah was utterly practical – no sermons, no spiritual pep-talks, but sleep and a square meal. If you're caring for someone in a depressed state, think how you can assist in simple, practical ways such as this. Never ignore the ordinary and the obvious. Feelings can often be dictated by a person's physical condition.

The power of touch

The Bible mentions how the angel touched Elijah and said, 'Get up and eat' (1 Kings 19:5). I believe the simple act of touching can be very significant. Physical touch conveys an enormous amount. The New Testament describes numerous occasions when Jesus touched people, including those suffering from leprosy. No ordinary person would have ever touched these outcasts. But Jesus was not afraid to touch. He laid hands on people; he sat children on his lap. Physical contact was part of his ministry.

My wife Polly and I have a strategy when either of us is feeling down. It's called 'Cuddles make things better.' To the logical, rational mind, it may seem naïve. But the human psyche doesn't respond merely to what is logical and rational. To touch

12 God's recovery plan

is to care. Such opportunities are inevitably more limited for the single person, but even if you are single it doesn't mean you must never touch or be touched. A big, affirming hug may not solve specific problems, but it helps your mind to cope. A depressed person can't manage complex prescriptions anyway. Simple, practical things are what is needed. Depressed people may scarcely have touched another human being for weeks. Warm, affectionate touch of a non-sexual nature is one way in which depressed people can be helped by supportive friends or partners. Research is increasingly showing how human touch generates a positive psychological response.

I read recently how babies who are deprived of their mother's touch within the first few hours of life tend to cry up to 500% more during their first three months. I believe that what is true for babies is true throughout life. We need tangible, demonstrative human affection. It's been shown that even stroking your pet can reduce your blood pressure.

Ironically, though, it is often depressed people who most fight shy of human contact. Natural inhibitions, Anglo-Saxon character traits and parental upbringing may make it hard for them. But here's another example of how a friend can provide the sort of help that depressed people can't provide for themselves. However embarrassed you may feel, don't draw back from putting your arm around their shoulder, touching their hand, squeezing their arm or giving them a hug. You may be the angel that God has sent, as he did with Elijah.

The second step in God's recovery plan for Elijah was to get him to face his actual circumstances, however distorted his viewpoint. 'What are you doing here, Elijah?' he asks (verses 9, 13). It wasn't meant as a rebuke. It was a gentle, probing question, to elicit some conversation from Elijah. When you are depressed, lectures don't help. They drive you further down. But God says, 'Come on. Tell me about it. Express how you feel.' And Elijah pours out a flood of frustrated feeling. 'Lord, I have been very zealous for you. I've been working so hard. But what good has it done? The situation hasn't changed a bit. I'm the only one left, and they're trying to get rid of me too' (see verses 10, 14).

Actually, he'd got it wrong. Things weren't what they seemed to him. There were seven thousand others who had stayed faithful to God (verse 18). But God didn't try and argue with him, or persuade him of the facts – at least, not at this stage.

Instead, God gave him a pictorial display of his power, with the storm, the earthquake and the fire. The lesson was simple: however awe-inspiring God's physical manifestations may have been on Mount Carmel in the presence of the prophets of Baal, Elijah was not to depend on these for his experience of God.

Signs and wonders are no substitute for an intimate personal relationship. So God was not in the wind, earthquake or fire. He spoke afterwards in the stillness (verses 11–12).

God provided a support partner

Christians today have become experts in frenzied and non-stop activity, and have lost the art of being still. Maybe we need to shed some of our commitments. In this same story, God said to Elijah, 'I'm going to send you back, but I'll give you a different job to do. I'm going to send you to find other people to do what you've been doing, to take the pressure off you' (see verses 15–16). In his mercy, God didn't require Elijah to go back and face Jezebel. 'No,' he said, 'I'll give you something else to do now, Elijah. And I'm going to give you a partner from now on, so you no longer have to minister alone.'

So Elijah was given a special helper, Elisha, to be alongside him, to stay with him, to share the spiritual load, to support him. That's what a depressed person needs. If you're concerned about friends with depression, God may wish you to be their Elisha, to support them and be alongside them. Their pride may prevent them from recognizing their need of such a person, or from wanting such support. You certainly don't want to be a nuisance, or interfering, but love sometimes needs to run the risk of rejection. That will not be easy, and you will need to pray that God will give you the right sensitivity. A depressed person may not find your role easy to accept. It can't have been easy for Elijah, but if you read on in 1 Kings, you discover how it put him back on his feet so that he could carry on an even more powerful ministry.

Is there a primary cause?

I don't know if Elijah was someone with a perfectionist streak in his make-up. I suspect he may have been. But what I have discovered is that those people whose lives are performance-oriented tend to be vulnerable to depression. Their emotional stamina eventually can't cope with the constant striving to achieve, to gain acceptance, to be loved and to avoid rejection. It shuts down from exhaustion and the disillusionment of realizing that all the effort seems to have been fruitless. Anger and an acute sense of injustice are the resulting emotions which, if not dealt with, can lead to depression.

David Seamands makes these two perceptive comments:

The most concise definition of depression I know is this: 'Depression is frozen rage' ... As surely as the night follows the day, depression follows unresolved, repressed, or improperly expressed anger.

He goes on to add:

I have rarely met a depressive perfectionist who didn't have a terrific sense of injustice and unfairness. The only answer to this deep anger against the injustices of life is forgiveness. Who most often needs to be forgiven? Parents and family members. So often, the roots of depression are buried in the subsoil of early family life. And unless you learn to deal honestly with those angry roots, to face your resentment and forgive, you'll be living in a greenhouse where depression is sure to flourish.[1]

Similarly, Dr John Lockley defines depression as 'inturned aggression'.[2] Not all experts accept this, but even if it is not the explanation in every case, it is worth exploring, so that an attempt can be made to deal with the cause rather than merely tackling the symptoms. Emotional pain can lie apparently dormant for years, and it may seem to have had very little effect on your life, but don't bet on it. I have written (in the chapters on anger) about how past memories can be dealt with. Some people argue that it is preferable to let sleeping dogs lie, and dredging up trauma from the past is counter-productive. Unfortunately, such memories rarely 'sleep'; they insidiously eat away at us subconsciously, and when the problem surfaces in the form of depression (or some other emotionally related illness) we may not even recognize where its origins lie.

Forgiveness, which is usually the key ingredient in healing of past memories, does not mean that you have to become 'wet' and tolerate sin. God isn't trying to turn you into a doormat. But it's the only effective way I know of coming to terms with the consequences of other people's sins. However you respond, you have to live with the consequences of other people's impact on you. But how much better if you don't have to live with pain as well! And forgiveness is the only way of stopping such pain. Even if the person who wronged you has long since died, or disappeared from your life, it is still possible to forgive them mentally and emotionally.

Forgiveness can be perhaps the most practical way for depressed people to begin the process of renewing their mind. It may well be excruciatingly hard. Depression itself does not respond to willpower. Thus it may not be possible to tackle it all at once. It may be necessary for drugs and medical treatment to have some effect first. Even then, forgiveness can take a long time.

By now, you may be feeling rather angry or frustrated if

nothing in this chapter seems applicable to you, or, worse, if it seems subtly damning or unhelpful. It certainly does a depressed person no good to be subjected to introspective examination, labelled, and prescribed spiritual remedies like aspirins. Every depressed person's deep valley of darkness is different. But sometimes a degree of bravery is needed to acknowledge the possibility that there is an unresolved issue that is giving rise to depression. Attributing all depression to biochemical imbalances can sometimes be a more acceptable alternative for us to believe, because it absolves us of all responsibility.

You are not necessarily to blame for your depression even if you do identify any factors which it lies within your power to change. But it does mean that you can look forward to the time when you can take greater responsibility for yourself as you are now, and as you eventually will be. It may take time, but it's worth waiting for. Here's where having a supportive friend and confidant(e) to consult can once again be helpful. Depression can cloud one's own objectivity. Such an impartial person may well be able to recognize if anything in this chapter makes some sense of the way you feel, even if it's not obvious to you. Ask them for an honest and non-judgmental opinion.

· Biochemical causes, circumstances in life, unresolved problems, temperament and mental illness can all bring about depression. But trying to diagnose the source on your own is never a wise course of action. Get a thorough medical assessment, and look for a trusted friend to support you on the road to recovery.

Above all, remember that your ultimate security is not in the way you feel, but in the knowledge that God's love for you is absolutely unchanging. Your relationship with God as one of his sons or daughters is never dependent on your feelings. It rests on God's unchanging love for you, because 'He chose us in him [Christ] before the creation of the world . . . In love he predestined us to be adopted as his sons through Jesus Christ' (Ephesians 1:4–5).

In my own period of depression, one of the few encouragements I clung on to was the reminder that however long it lasted, it would not be permanent. Psalm 23 speaks of 'walking through' the valley of the shadow of death; in Isaiah 43:2, God's promise is: 'When you pass through the waters, I will be with you . . . When you walk through the fire, you will not be burned.' Almost more reassuring than the guarantee of God's presence (which I couldn't feel anyway), was the promise that I would not be stuck in the flood, the fire and the valley of the shadow for ever; I would pass through them.

Faith, in these circumstances, may simply be the dogged determination to hang on to God when logic, common sense and feelings all tell you it's futile. The prophet Micah who, it seems, may have struggled with depression himself, expressed such faith and determination when he wrote:

> Though I have fallen, I will rise.
> Though I sit in darkness,
> the LORD will be my light.
> (Micah 7:8)

Martin Luther, another illustrious Christian who fell prey to depression, had the same mindset when he penned these lines:

> Feelings come and feelings go,
> And feelings are deceiving.
> My warrant is the Word of God;
> Naught else is worth believing.
>
> Though all my heart should feel condemned
> For want of some sweet token,
> There is One greater than my heart
> Whose Word cannot be broken.

12 God's recovery plan

I'll trust in God's unchanging Word
  Till soul and body sever;
For though all things shall pass away,
  His Word shall stand for ever!

Notes

1. David Seamands, *Healing for Damaged Emotions* (Victor Books, 1981), p. 125.
2. Dr John Lockley, *A Practical Workbook for the Depressed Christian* (Word, 1991), p. 129.

For personal study or group discussion

1. Why do you think that many Christians who read the Bible and pray still have problems with depression?
2. Why did Elijah feel depressed? Why didn't his triumphant victory over the prophets of Baal prove to be an effective buffer against depression?
3. Do you agree that perfectionists and performance-oriented people tend to be prone to depression? Why?
4. Can ongoing depression be linked to unresolved anger? In what way?
5. What steps would you take to try to help a depressed person?

13. Guilt: a crippling problem

Flicking through the pages of Ceefax, the BBC's teletext information service, I came across this interesting item:

UK TOPS THE LEAGUE IN FEELING GUILTY

Guilt is a British disease which could be threatening the nation's health, a group of scientists has said. A study showed that 41% of people in the UK would enjoy everyday pleasures more if they did not feel guilty. The study examined attitudes in eight countries to 13 pleasures including eating chocolate and watching TV. While the UK came second in the overall 'pleasure league', it was above average when it came to feeling guilty.[1]

Taken at face value, one might conclude from that clip that all guilt is harmful and serves to undermine the quality and enjoyment of life. A moment's reflection will bring the

13 Guilt: a crippling problem

realization that that isn't true. Without guilt, there is every possibility that we would degenerate into amoral, depraved animals, indulging in all manner of cruelty, deceit and sin with no form of discipline or corrective. As we have seen, feelings themselves are neither good nor bad. It is the appropriateness of them to the circumstances that determines whether what we are experiencing is healthy or not. Guilt can serve as a very helpful motivator in changing my behaviour. Equally, it can be a crippling prison of condemnation and torment.

According to Sigmund Freud, guilt is simply a conditioned response, which can be resolved by self-knowledge and self-acceptance. What Freud failed to acknowledge is that the universe has a moral structure, and that guilt is not merely an irrational projection of our unconscious mind. Guilt is designed by God to be a restraining and redeeming influence on fallen humanity. At times, however, something can go wrong, and guilt can become a handicap rather than a help.

One of my great interests is aviation. A recent television film told the true story of a pilot who had to fly a tiny crop-spraying Cessna 188 aircraft from California across the vast Pacific Ocean, to deliver it to a customer in Australia. It was only after flying for fourteen hours over mile after mile of empty ocean that the pilot realized that something had gone seriously wrong with his compass. His fuel reserves were low and he had no idea where he was. The film demonstrated how an Air New Zealand flight crew on a DC-10 jetliner managed to trace him and lead him to a safe landing, in darkness, with only a few drops of fuel left in his tanks.

Human beings are like aircraft in that they also have a type of inbuilt compass. We call it our conscience. It's a very delicate instrument. Its function is to give us a kind of pointer to whether we are going right or wrong. I heard David Watson state that the most powerful and effective preacher in the world is the human conscience. It's something that is unique to the human race. There isn't an animal or any other creature on this planet that has a conscience. But while your conscience can be a tremendous blessing in guiding, warning and protecting you, it can also torment, disturb and nag. The powerful influence of one's conscience can lead to depression, despair, neurotic illness and sometimes even to suicide.

It's been there right from the very beginning. In the Garden of Eden, what was it that Adam and Eve were suffering from? A bad conscience! What did Joseph's brothers suffer from, when Joseph revealed himself to them as a top Egyptian official, years after they had sold him into slavery? A bad conscience. What did David suffer from when Nathan the prophet came and challenged his adultery? Again, a bad conscience.

But, as with that little Cessna 188's compass, our conscience can turn out to be a most inaccurate guide to the course we need to steer through life. This is because our conscience is not the voice of God. It is certainly a means by which we can receive the voice of God. But conscience can be affected by all sorts of different factors – by our upbringing, by our society, by our education, as well as by our own desires. An infant does not come into this world clutching a set of God's standards for behaviour. Whatever that child is taught by its parents becomes the norm: what is right and wrong, acceptable and not acceptable. And like an aircraft compass, our conscience needs to be regularly checked, tested and constantly reset if we're going to steer a straight course through life. Most of us have a conscience that is too conditioned by the way we were brought up, and the things we feel guilty about are what our parents or teachers taught us to feel guilty about.

When we become adults, there is another factor that tends to shape and influence our conscience significantly. The mass media have more impact than perhaps any other social factor, particularly in the realm of sexuality. Sexuality is part of God's will for the human race, and he created it good and to be enjoyed, within the boundaries he set. But stage by stage, the media have conditioned people to consider promiscuity acceptable. James

13 Guilt: a crippling problem

Bond succeeds in getting every pretty girl under the shower or between the sheets on every possible occasion. Once that kind of activity no longer raised any eyebrows, homosexuality then became acceptably portrayed by the media, and today spouse-swapping and group sex are considered trendy pastimes. These things have become increasingly glamorized through the media. How many people now watch programmes on television which would have shocked and scandalized them twenty years ago? The gradual conditioning has been very effective. Our consciences get numbed by constant exposure to the wrong influences, and we end up with consciences tuned to what the mass media are feeding us.

But however distorted or inaccurate your conscience is, it's very difficult to silence it totally. As Lady Macbeth found to her cost, even the most concerted efforts to wipe out the marks of guilt aren't always effective. There is nothing more persistent and indelible on the human mind than a troubled conscience.

One might have thought that in a generation which has shed moral absolutes, and considers permissiveness to be a sign of maturity, our society would be free from feelings of guilt and all the accompanying mental and physical problems. But this is anything but the case. Guilt is one of today's most crippling problems. Psychiatrists and therapists have sometimes said that more than half their patients could be cured tomorrow if they could overcome their real or imaginary guilt, But there is no such man-made guilt eradicator on the market. You cannot deal with guilt with ECT, or with antidepressants and tranquillizers. There's only one way that guilt can be dealt with – by cleansing and forgiveness from God himself.

My colleague Bob Love shared with me this week about how a man had come to see him during a weekend conference. Overcome by emotion, he confessed, 'I've got so much in my past that I can't see God ever forgiving me.' He went on to describe how he had served as a soldier in the Vietnam war, and had frequently interrogated captured Vietnamese soldiers. One method he had employed was to bundle the captured soldier into a plane, take off and, at a height of several thousand feet, open up the door and dangle the prisoner out of the plane. If the prisoner was unable or unwilling to supply the required information, he would simply let go and watch him hurtle, screaming, to his death. He had done this more than once. Now, twenty years or more later, he found that he couldn't live with himself for guilt.

Bob gently reminded him that Christ can forgive. 'Christ died for you just as you are. Even though you did terrible things, the cross is the place where God can forgive you.' He laid hands on the man who, with tears, pleaded for God's forgiveness and mercy. The next day, Bob reported, there had been the most amazing change. The man's face was radiant. He said, 'It's a miracle. I never thought God could accept me.'

Not everyone has a past like that. But that man is not untypical in the way that guilt was emotionally eating away at him within. I counted up today the number of people who have shared with me in the past week that they feel guilty about something. There was the person who came to see me burdened by a periodic failure to be sexually moral. Guilt was causing this sad soul to wonder if it was right to continue going to church. Not long afterwards, while I was visiting a home where there had been a bereavement, the daughter in the family admitted to frequent 'guilt-trips', regretting things she had said to her late mother, and wishing she had done certain things differently.

A member of my congregation became the third example in as many days when he confessed to feeling guilt about the level of his financial giving to the church. And today I counselled a young man brought up by demanding and perfectionist parents who constantly made him feel guilty. He perpetually felt that he was letting them down. If he didn't dance to their tune, he was emotionally blackmailed to make him feel guilty. Small wonder that when he shares his understandable emotional pain with friends, he feels guilty for burdening them. When his friends don't know how to handle such raw emotions, it compounds his guilt.

The strange thing is that despite the widespread nature of the problem, guilt has received very little attention in recent years. Even in the church it is not acknowledged as much as it once was. There's a truncated gospel doing the rounds which emphasizes God's love, and how Jesus can help us and heal us and meet our needs. But the necessity of dealing with sin and wrongdoing, and how we get our consciences cleansed from guilt, are issues that tend to have become neglected.

Some of the examples above illustrate genuine guilt for specific wrongdoing. Other are examples of false guilt, when individuals perceive that they have failed or done wrong, even when in fact they have done the best they can. But in either case, the feeling of guilt is still very real, and is plaguing their lives.

Why, they ask, can't we just put these things behind us and get on with life? In fact, that is the normal way that most people try to deal with whatever it is that they feel ashamed of or embarrassed about. After all, they rationalize, other people have done worse things. And yet, for many, the feeling of guilt lingers on. If they try to banish it from their minds, or hide from the past, they never quite manage it. Even those who have become Christians, and can confidently share the message of forgiveness with others, not uncommonly have something in their own past about which they still feel guilty. There's something that they cannot forget. My study has frequently been the place where mature Christians of many years' standing have unburdened stories of sexual indiscretion, abortion and countless other sins which were continuing to plague them. Even if in some sense they felt that God had forgiven them, it quickly became apparent that they felt unable to forgive themselves.

Dealing with the roots of guilt

It is here that it becomes crucial to distinguish between genuine guilt and false guilt. Genuine guilt is the result of a wrong act or attitude. It is dealt with by admitting our sin to God in repentance and receiving his promised forgiveness. Genuine guilt should never be ignored or put on the back burner. It's God's way of alerting us to something that needs dealing with in our lives.

Guilt, and the sin which causes it, is rather like household rubbish. We have to dispose of it regularly and repeatedly. When we don't, the whole house starts stinking. In our house we have a small flip-top waste bin near the kitchen sink which gets filled up about twice a week. In our former home, it was simply a case of taking it outside and depositing it in the wheelie-bin by the gate. We now live in a 'black bag' area. There are no wheelie-bins. We have to remember to tip all our rubbish into a black bag on Tuesday evenings and put it out on the pavement on Wednesday morning. If we forget, we're stuck with that rubbish for another week. We can't leave it outside, as the local yobs regularly rip open the bag, smash the bottles and scatter rubbish and broken glass far and wide. So the black bag has to stay inside and we have to try to hide it away somewhere where it won't taint the whole house with a bad smell. (And if anyone from my local council is reading this, can we please have some wheelie-bins?)

Some people's inner lives are like houses where the rubbish is never taken out. It just accumulates and starts stinking and getting inconvenient. But Jesus wants to wipe the slate clean. If we only had the sense to take it out regularly and dump the stuff! If stored household rubbish is a nuisance, sin and guilt that remain stored are even more of a nuisance. Why hang on to it when God is willing to set us free, and forgive freely, instantly and continually? There's nothing to be gained by heaping up bigger and bigger mounds of emotional garbage. Dump it at the cross. Don't allow sin and guilt to pile up over long periods of time. The Bible's message is repeatedly couched in terms like this: 'If we confess our sins, he [God] is faithful and just and will forgive us our sins and purify us from all unrighteousness' (1 John 1:9).

13 Guilt: a crippling problem

Some people find that free forgiveness sounds just too good to be true. It might be true for someone else, but not for them – they've been too bad. They are too undeserving; what they have done is too terrible for Christ to forgive. After all, it goes against all the rules of justice and fair play to have done all those things and then go scot-free. This is one of the subtleties of guilt. Our mind tells us that we deserve to pay for the things we've done wrong. And feeling guilty is one way of paying which we impose on ourselves. Even if Christ forgives us, there can sometimes be something in us which doesn't want to forgive ourselves. Guilt can be a self-imposed punishment, a penance for whatever it is we've done that has disgusted and shamed us.

Yet it is entirely unnecessary, because the bill has already been paid. Two thousand years ago, on a hill called Calvary, the sinless Jesus took the sum total of the world's sin and guilt – past, present and future – on himself. Including yours. There are no exceptions. Adultery is included, abortion is included – whatever it is that you're most ashamed of is included. If we try to contribute by paying some miserable penance of guilt, then we are insulting God.

The word-processor on which I do my writing was given to me as a very generous gift by a friend several years ago. It was a vast improvement on the pre-war battered portable typewriter I used in Africa. But supposing that when this marvellous gift was delivered to me, I had reached into my pocket and said to my friend, 'Look, I can see this is a very expensive gift. It has obviously entailed a good deal of sacrifice on your part. Let me give you something towards it – some contribution to its cost.' Can you imagine anything more insulting? And yet sometimes we dare to come to Jesus and say, 'Thank you, Jesus, that you died for my sins. Now please can I add a little bit of my own guilt, so that I feel I'm at least paying something of the penalty myself?'

David Seamands writes: 'The first step toward Christian adulthood is to be done with any subtle form of inner penance and self-condemnation for already forgiven and forgotten sins. The guilty self needs to become the forgiven self.'[2]

If we are continuing to carry a load of guilt for something we have done, then perhaps we are insulting our Saviour. It is unnecessary, because Jesus Christ has already paid the cost in full. This doesn't mean that God dispenses cheap forgiveness. It is the most costly thing in the world. Nor does it give us licence to trade on God's mercy by carrying on doing wrong. What it does mean is that once we have repented and asked God to forgive us and wipe the slate clean, we can be guilt-free. Is that good news or what? That's why Christians have got something to smile about. How many people avoid church because they think that they will feel guilty if they go there? In reality, the church is the one place that will tell them how to get rid of it. As somebody once put it, 'Jesus came not to rub it in, but to rub it out.'

Notes

1. An international study from Associates for Research Into the Science of Enjoyment, reported on BBC Ceefax News Service, 7 November 1996.
2. David Seamands, *Putting Away Childish Things* (Victor Books, 1982), p. 138.

14. Erasing false guilt

In the light of the previous chapter, the remedy for real guilt is quite straightforward. But what about false guilt? False guilt is often more difficult to identify so clearly. It is a feeling, which may not even be tied to a specific event at all, of self-condemnation and unease. Morbid and introspective self-examination can generate false guilt. Christians need to learn to distinguish between the Holy Spirit's action in convincing them of sin, and the tormenting accusations of the devil. The ministry of the Spirit is always specific and precise, whereas Satan makes sweeping and generalized charges against us.

A Christian student wrote to me a while ago, saying, 'I don't want to tell you, or anyone, about all the struggle and the setback which I am going through. But if I don't tell, it might just eat me alive . . . If I ever ask why I must shed my tears alone, the answer comes back that it is my own fault.' I discovered that so much false guilt had accumulated in this young woman that she even considered that she was in some way responsible for the starving millions in the famine-ravaged parts of the Third World.

False guilt can occur in Christians when they refuse to believe and accept that they're forgiven, rather than because they are somehow refusing to seek it. I have repeatedly had to reassure Christians who keep responding to appeals to commit their lives to Christ, confessing their sins time and time again, because they still don't 'feel' forgiven. Their sin, if any, is in a failure to accept forgiveness, rather than a failure to seek it. They will not forgive themselves.

Another situation where false guilt occurs is when our consciences become too active. A biblical example of this occurred in the church at Corinth, when some of the new converts expressed qualms about eating meat that had been sacrificed to idols. Since virtually all the meat available in the Corinthian marketplace had come straight from the pagan Corinthian temples, some of the Christians wondered if this was perhaps grounds for vegetarianism. But when Paul wrote to them he pointed out that since the idols were nothing more than man-made representations of non-existent gods, there was no reason to feel any concern about eating meat sacrificed in such a way.

Sometimes true and false guilt can get mixed up together. An earnest and enthusiastic young man in a church I pastored in Africa felt very guilty about playing tennis. Such guilt would seem utterly misplaced to anybody else. But this young man had idolized the game before his conversion to Christ. As a rising star on the local tennis circuits, he played seven days a week, and tennis became his god. He worshipped tennis, morning, noon and night. Given that background, it becomes easier to understand his guilt at indulging in his former 'idolatry' after he became a Christian. When his conscience alerted him to the danger of allowing his former obsession to take first place in his life, it was fulfilling a true and positive function. But the false guilt was the temporary, mistaken belief that the game of tennis itself was wrong, for him or anyone else.

My hope was that this was a short-lived phase, and that as he grew stronger in his faith, he would come to see that tennis need not be anything sinful, provided it didn't rule and dominate his life. But I certainly wouldn't condemn him in those early months of his Christian commitment for feeling guilty every time he picked up a tennis racket. His newly awakened conscience was flashing danger signals, and I believe he was right to take notice of that. There was still a rival bid for the affections of his heart and the commitment of his will.

Perhaps it would have been a sin for him to play tennis in those early days. But it certainly isn't a sin for other people. And there are all sorts of things which people can feel guilty about. It may be true guilt in some people, but false guilt in others. Numerous parents feel guilty about not spending enough time with their children. That indicator from their conscience might be accurate with some, but producing false guilt in others.

If their consciences become *too* active, the result is that they feel guilty not only for not spending enough time with the children, but also for not answering the telephone when they *are* spending time with their children. They are literally damned if they do and damned if they don't. Whatever choice they make, their conscience will find something to niggle about.

When our consciences are oversensitive, or inaccurate, then we can end up emotionally whipping ourselves with false guilt. The cause is usually that our consciences have been overly conditioned by our parents, our society or the type of education we received. Legalistic homes and churches which put an undue emphasis on rules and discipline, dos and don'ts, tend to breed people with hypersensitive consciences and resultant emotional damage.

Invalid guilt can be the constant companion of those with a perfectionist mindset. The cause is not deliberate wrongdoing, but everyday human shortcomings. The solution lies in having the ready ability to forgive ourselves, alongside the recognition that only God is perfect. And while God is perfect, he is not a perfectionist. His acceptance of us is not conditional on our performance or our worthiness. God does not harbour unrealistic expectations or demand impossible performance. If he believed that we were capable of perfection, he would not have needed to send Jesus.

If perfectionism and self-punishing guilt have slowly taken root in your life since childhood, don't expect to experience change overnight. Getting rid of the constant self-deprecation and low self-esteem which reinforce false guilt comes about only by the process of renewing our minds. And unlearning bad habits can take longer than acquiring good habits. But as we increasingly grasp the wonder of God's incredible and unconditional acceptance of us, we shall find that, bit by bit, we cease to be plagued by false guilt.

There is, however, damage of another kind in childhood that can induce terribly crippling false guilt in an adult. This is the horrendous damage caused by sexual abuse. I have a letter written to me a few years back by a woman in her twenties who preferred to remain anonymous. With heart-rending honesty she wrote:

My new life in Christ is continually blighted by the guilt of what has happened to me in the past . . . for when I was a child I was sexually abused. For many years I have tried to ignore this problem, but now it is becoming more and more real as I am forced to see the damage that has been done. Sometimes the realization that I have sexual feelings and desires sickens and horrifies me. For to admit that is to admit a link, a similarity, between myself and the person who abused me. Rationally, I know that sex is something beautiful which God has created, but somehow I can never get my feelings to agree with my mind . . . I feel vaguely guilty at my own inability to cope with life.

One might wonder why a person should feel guilty as a result of some perverted act that was inflicted upon her at the age of twelve. Perhaps it's because such molesting began to awaken her own sexual feelings at that young age. Perhaps in some cases it is because, despite hating the perpetrator, the person began to enjoy the feelings of arousal. But, as David Seamands comments, 'one of the most basic steps in finding freedom from unnecessary guilt is to distinguish between taking responsibility for our own sins and refusing to take it for the sins done against us by other people'.[1]

There are therefore all sorts of factors that can give rise to false guilt. Whether our sense of guilt is valid or not needs to be measured first of all by what the Bible has to say. Even if the issue is not referred to directly, there may be an underlying principle. The Bible doesn't directly tell us to pay our electricity bill or ensure that our car is properly taxed, but it does tell us not to steal (Exodus 20:15; Ephesians 4:28) and to pay our taxes (Romans 13:7). The principles in those cases are not too hard to find, and it is wrong to attempt to deaden our conscience on these points by rationalizing our circumstances.

In other situations, direction from the Bible is harder to discover. Christians have come to different conclusions over such questions as whether a Christian should practise birth control or drink alcohol. Masturbation is something that is never mentioned in the Bible, and yet it's one of the biggest sources of guilt among many Christians. Masturbation is frequently accompanied by sexual fantasy. Are such fantasies always wrong? If they generate lust, then according to the Bible, yes. If masturbation gains an addictive grip on us, clearly yes again. But where this is not the case, Christians are far from unanimous in their answers, because the Bible doesn't seem to offer precise definitions.

Where the Bible doesn't appear to offer any light on the subject, the next step might be to explore the values and standard of your parents. If your conscience troubles you over something that you suspect might not actually be wrong, check out what you learned in childhood. Similarly, if you don't feel at all troubled about something that seems to horrify other Christians, it might well be worth asking yourself some questions to see whether your conscience got distorted at some point.

In trying to align our consciences to 'true North' on issues where the Bible doesn't make any clear statement, it's usually helpful to ask, 'Would this honour God? Would he feel comfortable about my doing this? Does this seem consistent with the fact that my body is the temple of the Holy Spirit?' This type of question can help to give your conscience appropriate and godly direction.

Having the right view of God

Of course, this presupposes that you have the right thinking about God in the first place. Or maybe it's the right feelings. The way some Christians feel about God can be very different from their doctrine or head-theology. When an overactive conscience has been exalted to represent infallibly the voice of God, then it's easy to think of God as the internal policeman, with truncheon at the ready, poised to pounce the moment we put a foot wrong. In those circumstances, the belief that God is both perfectly just and perfectly loving can be a difficult balance to maintain. Too many people make do with second-best because of the mistaken feeling that this is what they deserve, and that God is punishing them for past sins. The image of God as an angry, condemnatory judge is a common one, and breeds a generation of people in bondage to guilt that grace and mercy can never seem to touch.

I'm also amazed at the number of Christians I encounter who feel guilty about something perfectly legitimate and wholesome – maybe a talent they possess, or a hobby they enjoy. Like the tennis-player I mentioned earlier, they have concluded that God wants them to give it up. Why? Because they enjoy it so much. It's almost impossible for them to believe that God is delighted when they enjoy themselves. If that enjoyment becomes an obstacle to their relationship with him, then yes, it must be dealt with. But God is not against people enjoying themselves!

The solution

Once again, it is helpful to adopt the three principles described in earlier parts of this book: repentance, repudiation, replacement.

Guilt, if it is genuine, is designed by God to bring about *repentance*. This provides the wonderful opportunity of knowing God's absolute and total forgiveness. Hebrews 4:16 tells us to 'approach the throne of grace with confidence, so that we may receive mercy and find grace to help us in our time of need'. God doesn't tell us to come with guilt, but with confidence. It's this assurance of God's mercy and grace that gives us grounds for knowing that our guilt has been conclusively dealt with.

If you suspect that the guilt you are feeling is actually false or unjustified, it may still be necessary to repent. Self-hatred and self-deprecation may not, in fact, be godly humility, but may rather indicate an inability to grasp God's unconditional acceptance. Has your mind fallen prey to the devil's lie that God has written you off as a lost cause? Repentance simply means to change your mind and your will, and this is often necessary even when you have not deliberately set out on the wrong course. A recognition that, however unwittingly, your mindset or your beliefs or your actions have been misguided is the essence of repentance. There must then follow the decision to change direction with God's help.

This is as true for your thought processes as it is for your actions. If your feelings about God have been at variance with his revelation of himself as a loving, merciful Father, then that needs a 'course correction', brought about by repentance. Perhaps repentance is needed not so much for failing to *seek* God's forgiveness as for failing to *accept* it. This may also involve repenting of an unforgiving attitude towards yourself – that self-imposed penance that tries to punish you for past mistakes. Accept yourself the same way that God does! One of the most helpful little sayings I ever memorized was this: 'God is not against you for your sins; he is for you against your sins.' There's no greater encouragement than knowing that.

The next step is therefore to *repudiate* and verbally cancel all the negative and self-belittling thoughts and attitudes that have multiplied as a consequence of your guilt. Comments such as 'I hate myself', 'I'm such a failure', 'I wish I were dead', 'I give up', I'm hopeless', are not consistent with how God feels about you. They are at variance with what the Bible teaches. We need to guard very carefully what we think and say about ourselves.

Finally, *replace* all such wrong expressions with the truth of God's Word. For example, insert your own name in the following sentences, which are based on the clear teaching of the Bible:

God says: 'I will forgive your wickedness, _____, and will remember your sins no more' (see Jeremiah 31:34).

There is now no condemnation for _____, who is in Christ Jesus (see Romans 8:1).

God says: 'I have chosen you, _____, and have not rejected you' (see Isaiah 41:9).

I, _____, am washed, I am sanctified, I am justified in the name of the Lord Jesus Christ and by the Spirit of our God (1 Corinthians 6:11).

Do persist with this, until you have effectively obliterated every invalid thought or attitude from your mind. Feelings need to correspond to the truth, and there is no better way of bringing them into line than by the constant and appropriate use of God's Word.

But ultimately, we must remember that dealing with unruly feelings and emotions should not depend on a technique, however biblical, but on a relationship. It is his redeeming grace that breaks the chains of the past, not our own mental exercises or psychological insights. It is likewise his reprogramming grace that can change the behaviour patterns of today, not our own self-discipline or resolve. These are all things that God can welcome and use, but on their own they have limited value. It is the power of his Spirit operating in a daily relationship with us which is the key to having a renewed mind. God may not wave a magic wand, but he is committed to a relationship whereby we are daily being 'transformed into his likeness with ever-increasing glory' (2 Corinthians 3:18).

Note

1. David Seamands, *Healing Grace* (Scripture Press, 1989), p. 139.

For personal study or group discussion

1. In confiding her misgivings about a sexual relationship, a young woman told me, 'I feel guilty about saying "no" to my boyfriend because I don't want to hurt him or make him feel rejected.' What would you say to her?
2. To what extent is our conscience an accurate reflection of the voice of God? Or has it been significantly shaped by our culture, family or society?
3. Is your guilt genuine, or is it unjustified? In either case, what action are you going to take?

15. Wholeness is for holiness

'Don't worry; be happy' has become a popular catchphrase in recent years – perhaps because it encourages the mistaken belief that if only we could get our unruly emotions sorted out and under control, then we would be automatically fulfilled. And the desire to get rid of what we consider to be negative emotions is often matched by the desire to experience the 'positive' ones. *The Reader's Digest* recently published a 'happiness test' for people to gauge their degree of happiness and pleasure in life. Society is now recognizing that despite all our modern technology and growing affluence, people are often less happy than their grandparents were. I have already mentioned the elusive feel-good factor, which politicians and advertisers alike claim to provide. As do some churches. Happiness, joy, fulfilment, peace and 'spiritual highs' are the blessings on offer. But however pleasurable these may be, the question needs to be asked: are these the things that are at the top of God's priority list? Should the pursuit of happiness be our primary goal?

The obsessive desire for, and pursuit of, pleasure (positive emotions) is known as hedonism, and it is clear from the Bible that to follow Christ will be incompatible with the pursuit of pleasure at all costs. Following Christ entails crucifying our sinful nature, which will inevitably be emotionally painful. Effort and conflict rarely feel good at the time.

What we need to be careful of, therefore, is that in our keenness to get rid of destructive emotions, we don't lose perspective. The motive needs to be holiness rather than happiness. Happiness is a byproduct rather than an end in itself. God's intention in helping us towards emotional wholeness is to help us to live right. The Bible highlights God's concern that we are saved not merely *from* something, but *for* holiness. It came as a revelation to me when God's priorities were described by someone as 'holiness in this life and happiness in the next'. We mistakenly tend to assume that it's the other way round.

Emotional wholeness is therefore not an end in itself, but a means to an end. Wholeness is for holiness, if I can coin a phrase. And on the road to holiness we will encounter disappointment, fear, hardship and sorrow. These are not to be avoided at all costs, because they are stepping-stones by which God leads us towards spiritual maturity. There's much truth in the old Arab proverb that 'All sunshine makes a desert'. The emotionally painful experiences of life are the stuff on which faith is nurtured. And our relationship to God is never dependent on feelings. It is dependent on faith. And faith is an act of will far more than an expression of emotion.

I am so grateful that God created us with the capacity to feel, because so many feelings are good and enjoyable. Even those which aren't can still be used by him to train us, mature us and transform us on the path of ever-increasing holiness. And as we grow in holiness in this life, we can look forward to the experience in the next when emotional fulfilment will be complete. God will wipe every tear from our eyes, and there will be no more mourning or crying (Revelation 21:4); but we will hear the invitation of Jesus: 'Come and share your master's happiness!' (Matthew 25:23). What a prospect to look forward to! What an incentive to partake of Christ's holiness now!